POETS ON THE PSALMS

POETS
ON THE PSALMS

TRINITY UNIVERSITY PRESS
San Antonio

"No Rapture: The Psalms and Restiveness," copyright 2004 Carl Phillips. Reprinted from *Coin of the Realm* with the permission of Graywolf Press, Saint Paul, Minnesota.

Alicia Ostriker, "Psalm and Anti-Psalm: A Personal Interlude," in *For the Love of God: The Bible As an Open Book* (New Brunswick, N.J.: Rutgers University Press, 2007).

David Citino, "I Shall Not Want: The 23rd Psalm Comes to Cleveland, Ohio," in *Paperwork* (Kent, Ohio: Kent State University Press, 2003). Reprinted with permission of Kent State University Press.

Daniel Tobin, "Lamentation, Poetry, and the Double Life," in *Tiferet* vol. 1, issue 1, January/February 2006.

Cover design by Karen Schober
Book design by BookMatters, Berkeley

♾ The paper used in this publication meets the minimum requirements of the American National Standard for Information Sciences—Permanence of Paper for Printed Library Materials, ANSI Z39.48-1992.

Library of Congress Cataloging-in-Publication Data
Poets on the Psalms / edited by Lynn Domina.
          p. cm.
     SUMMARY: "This collection of essays interprets the Psalms as poetry. Written by fourteen acclaimed poets, the essays approach the Psalms from a personal, often autobiographical perspective" —Provided by publisher.
     Includes bibliographical references and index.
     ISBN 978-1-59534-047-4 (hardcover : alk. paper)
     ISBN 978-1-59534-048-1 (pbk. : alk. paper)
     1. Poets, American—Religious life.
     2. Bible. O.T. Psalms—Influence.
     3. Bible. O.T. Psalms—Criticism, interpretation, etc.
     4. Bible as literature.
     5. American essays.
     I. Domina, Lynn.
     PS129.P62   2008
     811'.009382232—dc22   2008000749

12   11   10   09   08   —   5   4   3   2   1

CONTENTS

INTRODUCTION

I'm a fond reader of books about the Bible, not professional theology so much as the responses, musings, speculations of ordinary readers. I feel reassured knowing that other readers would hightail it out of Nineveh, too, even if they risked tumbling head-first into the belly of a whale. I'm glad to know that many of us empathize with Lot's wife as she looks back, regardless of her particular reason. And surely I'm not the only one who envies Peter his impulsiveness, at least on the occasion when he jumps from his boat into the sea and splashes toward Jesus, newly risen and grilling breakfast on the shore. Often, walking the dog or mowing the lawn, I mull over these stories, peculiar and puzzling as they are. Sometimes, though, I'm stopped short by a single line from a canticle—"my spirit rejoices in God my savior," "receive your servant in peace"—or from a psalm—"Oh, God, come to my assistance." I suspect that various psalms are among the most often memorized portions of the Bible, and that the opening of Psalm 23, "The Lord is my shepherd," is the most quoted line, with the possible exception of "In the beginning . . ."

One evening a few years ago, I reclined in my study, enveloped in solitude, and thumbed through an anthology of essays by contemporary writers who each addressed one book of the Bible. I wish someone would edit a collection of essays written by poets about the Psalms, I thought. Someone, of course, quickly identified herself, as I realized that waiting around for someone else to read my mind would be, at best, foolish. So I thought about the many poets whose work indicated that they might be interested in contributing an essay, I looked up their addresses, and I sent out a couple dozen letters. That in itself was quite fun, for I'd been reading and loving the work of many of these contributors for years;

other contributors had published their first collections shortly before I began this project, and I decided that the abundance of first books addressing religious concerns must certainly be a sign.

When the completed essays began to arrive in my mailbox, I was astonished at both their quality and their range. The Psalms themselves, of course, display a range of emotions—rage, gratitude, grief, awe, fear. The speakers describe victory and defeat, security and humiliation. Their words instruct, challenge, reassure. The essays collected here reveal how pertinent the Psalms remain to men and women alive in the twenty-first century. The writers recalled the Psalms as they cared for elderly parents, as they drove across the country, as they composed their own poems.

These fourteen essays are arranged to reflect on each other's central concerns. If we all feel some familiarity with the Psalms, members of formal religious communities spend a comparatively substantial portion of each day praying the Psalms; in her opening essay, Madeline DeFrees recalls her life as a nun, its influence on her understanding of the Psalms, and their influence on her own poetry. In the three following essays, by Carl Phillips, Alicia Ostriker, and Jill Alexander Essbaum, the poets take on topics that can seem, to contemporary readers, at odds with some conventional religious views of life. Then, Enid Dame discusses Psalm 22 and its recitation by Jesus at his death while simultaneously examining the ways in which Christianity may and may not encourage anti-Semitism. Pattiann Rogers describes the relationship of particular psalms to specific poems of her own, connecting then with now. Catherine Sasanov, David Citino, and Angie Estes respond to Psalm 23, perhaps the best-known and best-loved poem in Jewish or Christian scripture; they each focus on the psalm's particular language and its significance to modern American culture. Diane Glancy and I consider place, the landscapes present in the Psalms and the landscapes we inhabit as we read and interpret them. Finally, essays by Robert Ayres, Janet McCann, and Daniel Tobin provide us with meditation and lamentations; Ayres, McCann, and Tobin find themselves mulling over particular psalms at crucial moments in their lives.

Finally, a note on translations. Several fine versions of the Psalms exist in English. Readers may be most familiar with the King James, or the New American, or the New Revised Standard Version of the Bible. Influenced by their own aesthetic preferences and denominational affiliations, the contributors to this collection also rely on various translations. Personally, I enjoy many of the slight distinctions made by these different translations as yet another point of entry into the Psalms.

This collection has been an extraordinary pleasure to put together; I trust that reading it will prove equally pleasurable.

THE SECRET LIFE OF POETRY AND THE PSALMS

Madeline DeFrees

> Keep me as the *apple* of the eye, hide me under
> the shadow of thy wings.
> —Psalm 17:8

Scorpios like to keep secrets. Although I don't put much stock in astrology, in this case, my stars have it right.

All my life I've enjoyed hiding things—even from myself—and the Psalms have often been my ally. In the convent, the Psalms were a bright thread woven through the texture of our days, from rising at 5:10 a.m. until lights out at 9:25 p.m. when we fell asleep, as often as not with some verse from the Psalms reverberating in our heads to prepare us for the next morning's meditation.

Although it has been nearly thirty years since I left the convent, waking or sleeping, a daily image from those years remains with me: It is late winter of 1937, and I am standing in the large dining room of the Oregon provincial house of the Sisters of the Holy Name of Jesus and Mary. My novice's habit is still new enough to generate mixed feelings of pride and disbelief. We are reciting the long Latin grace after dinner. At a signal from the presider, the postulants lead the way out of the refectory toward the chapel on the second floor. Walking slowly, two by two, we novices follow, and the professed Sisters fall in behind. The hall outside the dining room is windowless, illumined only by the white flash of novices' veils and small nightlights placed at intervals along the baseboards. As we walk, we recite Psalm 50, "The Miserere," in Latin, one side intoning the versicles, the other the responses. *Miserere mei, Deus, secundum magnam misericordiam tuam.* Have mercy on me, O God, according to thy great mercy.

Our hands, on this, as on all formal occasions, are hidden within the serge outer sleeves, which function almost like a muff. Something about this posture feels like a gradual disappearance into a comforting anonymity. Of all the convent rituals, this procession is my favorite vanishing act: the mingled voices in a language not my own, the long line of black-robed figures ahead and behind, the uniformity of dress and deportment combine to efface the differences and provide the illusion of belonging.

The slow procession emerges into light. Several of the older Sisters drop out of line to take the elevator. The others mount the stairs, paced by the psalm: *Ecce enim veritatem dilexisti incerta et occulta sapientiae tuae manifestasti mihi.* For behold thou hast loved truth: the uncertain and *hidden* things of thy wisdom thou hast made manifest to me (emphasis added).

At the chapel, we file into our assigned places but remain standing, waiting for the signal to genuflect. Then a few more prayers, led by the presider, and the clapper tells us to genuflect and file out, downstairs to the novitiate for the younger members, to the community room on the chapel floor for the others. Each group will gather in its respective room for Recreation of Rule.

Three times a day, all through our training period, we went to the chapel for the Little Office of the Blessed Virgin, consisting almost entirely of psalms. After our first vows, when we were teaching, this public prayer would be recited only on Saturday evenings, Sundays, and holy days and on special feast days of the congregation. When one of the Sisters died, the community assembled at the provincial house for the Office of Requiem. Add to these many encounters with the Psalms their daily use in the Proper of the Mass and the recitation of the "De Profundis" (Psalm 129) at 8 p.m. every evening, when the exterior convent bell rang.

Because the congregation was founded in French Canada, its official language sometimes grated on our ears. In a sea of Frenchified English (e.g., "they shall not 'tutoyer' one another") and syrupy hymns or the tortured syntax of bad translations, Latin was a mercy, and the Psalms a life raft.

Rereading the Psalms at this distance, I see that they fed my spiritual life in two ways: They sent an underground current deep through the forest of the unconscious that renewed the reservoirs of my poetry; and they helped me to hide the differences that kept me from belonging, at the same time that they preserved them intact.

In *Bread in the Wilderness*, Thomas Merton writes: "It must be admitted that the individual vocation to contemplative prayer is conditioned by individual temperament, and that there will always be souls who will usually find a deeper conscious peace and absorption in the presence of God when they are silent and alone than when they are praying in choir" (47).[1] Such was the case with me. It was easy to chant the Office on automatic, especially in Latin, while I went searching for the hidden God. Merton had added that the secret of the Psalter was the total gift of oneself to God, a gift that implies "a pure faith and an intense desire of love and above all, a firm hope of finding God hidden in his revealed word" (47–48).

The idea of a hidden God appealed to me, no doubt because of my own proclivity for hiding. This habit had begun early in childhood. My orphan mother, who had married at sixteen and lost her first daughter a few months after birth, turned to me to satisfy her unfulfilled needs. I was too young to respond as she wished and built defenses to keep her at a distance. On the surface I appeared docile and obedient, but, hidden away in the attic, safely removed from the family, I vented my negative feelings.

It's entirely predictable, then, that the first time I converted a psalm to poetic capital, I turned to the "De Profundis":

> Out of the depths I cry to you, O Lord,
>   Lord, hear my voice!
> Let your ears be attentive
>   to my voice in supplication—
> If you, O Lord, mark iniquities,
>   Lord, who can stand?
> But with you is forgiveness,
>   That you may be revered.

The words of the psalm were familiar as my own name. The cry arose from the secret depths, and I liked the fact that the action was situated on the margins of society. Here is the opening stanza of "Skid Row," first published in 1956:

> Out of the depths have I cried, O Lord,
> Where the lean heart preys on the hardened crust,
> Where short wicks falter on candle hopes
> And winter whips at a patchwork trust.

In "Whitsunday Office" (1964), the speaker is actually chanting the Office, while hearing it for the first time in English. Although I loved the Latin liturgies, I realized that community members who had not been "schooled in an ancient language" felt encouraged to participate more actively when the Office was in English. The speaker says:

> In choir I stand
> one with my sisters now at journey's end
> and hear, antiphonal, the chant break like a bell,
> leap through the chapel vault,
> spiral and somersault,
> with here and there a crack
> to make the music sweeter
> for a happy fault.

The poem comes to an end with these lines:

> One glass the less to see through darkly
> brings the image near.

"Psalm for a New Nun" appeared in 1967. I had mentioned to Carolyn Kizer that some of the nuns were letting their hair grow, to prepare for the possibility that the habit might be altered or abandoned. She thought that the topic would make a great poem. At first, I dismissed the idea, but the next morning when I opened my missal to prepare for the day's Mass, I was confronted by Psalm 124: "My life was rescued as a bird from the fowler's snare."

Although I can no longer locate the translation I found in the missal I was using then, I am sure that, as with the "De Profundis" poem, I repeated the words from the psalm verbatim as my opening line. Here is the first couplet:

My life was rescued as a bird from the fowler's snare.
It comes back singing tonight in my loosened hair

and proceeds to the end when the psalm again provides the text, with
the addition of two other words:

Broken is the snare and I am freed,
My help is in the name of the Lord who made
heaven and earth. Yes, earth.

The poem does change the psalm from first-person plural to first-person
singular.

In a 1972 poem titled "Living by the Water," I borrowed from Psalm
136 (137 in the King James), where language and image produce a poetry
I consider unrivaled:

By the streams of Babylon
    we sat and wept
On the aspens of that land
    we hung up our harps.
. . . .
How could we sing a song of the Lord
    in a foreign land?

In my poem, the second stanza contains the passage derived from
the psalm:

        When we slept, dry-eyed
on the shores of Babylon, how did we
hang our harp on the willow branch in this
strange land? Pale reed
beside the water, my water-sign
a wand depending on the hidden spring.

What the poem recalls to me now is the acute sense of exile I felt
when I received the community newsletter and found no mention of
those of us living and working apart from the group at a time when such
forays were infrequent.

Eventually, that water-sign and the magic wand it waved over the
hidden spring of poetry let me know that I didn't belong in the convent.

The camouflage of protective coloration had kept my differences hidden for some thirty-seven years. After my mother's death, I had gone on being the docile child, but events let me know, the inexorable way events do, that it was time to move on. All those differences so readily preserved by the rituals of conformity were still intact, and all I needed to do was stop hiding them, take my place in the world, and get on with the poems.

NOTES

1. Thomas Merton, *Bread in the Wilderness* (New York: New Directions, 1953).

ON RESTIVENESS—
IN ART, IN LIFE

The Psalms

Carl Phillips

To be human is to know—within oneself as well as in the relationship of the self to society at large—contradiction, or a conflict of several competing interests. We want what we can't have, or shouldn't have, or have been told we shouldn't want. In short, we have instinct. But what distinguishes humans from animals is an awareness of that instinct and of its possibilities, if left unchecked. Or perhaps another way to see it is that humans have, among their many instincts, an instinct to reconcile contradiction. Hence, the creation of laws, mortality, religion, and other means of giving some generally agreed-upon boundaries to human behavior.

If the artist is human, what makes the artist unique among humans is a seeming unwillingness to reconcile contradiction. I say "seeming," because finally it's less a matter of unwillingness than of inability. Since inability is not correctable (as opposed to unwillingness, which is susceptible to persuasion, whether in the form of punishment or of pleasure), it's not surprising that artists are the first to be held suspect within society—original artists, I mean. For it is the original artist who—again, because of an inability to do any differently—will always challenge rather than reinforce societal convention. This originality means from the start a unique way of seeing the world and of expressing that vision; and convention is not about uniqueness, but about conformity. The artist is at one moment dangerously intransigent (Dickinson's soul refusing, for example, to accept any society but her own), at the next moment frustratingly flippant (Whitman's "Do I contradict myself? / Very well, then, I contradict myself, / I am large, I contain multitudes"). An inability to speak in harmony with received tradition easily translates into a refusal to do so—into a hostility *toward* that tradition.

For the artist, there is less an impulse to reconcile contradiction than to plumb and sound contradiction's depths; and the result (given luck, gift, and vision) can be an art that refreshingly deepens and enlarges the beliefs and sensibilities of the very society it—inevitably, necessarily—also threatens.

◆ ◆ ◆

Maybe it has to do with my being a poet; or perhaps with my being biracial (that is, the product of a relationship that, in 1959, was in many parts of the United States illegal, and in every part unconventional); or my being gay might also figure here, given how vexed an issue homosexuality—like miscegenation—remains to this day, civil rights and Stonewall notwithstanding. Whatever the reasons, I have always been powerfully drawn toward the contradictory. It brings with it the unexpected; and the surprise of the unexpected may be pleasing or painful, but it will never be tedious—which is the business of perfection.

To allow for contradiction is, it seems to me, to be more honestly human; or perhaps the most human of contradictions is that between the instinct to reconcile contradiction and the temptation to yield to the contradictory. The reason the Greek tragedies still resonate with meaning is that they offer an honesty that has to do not with the absolute and consolidated nobility of the characters but with the unexpected unraveling of that nobility—and it's a ragged nobility that I am after.

One of my parents was raised as a Southern Baptist; the other, in the Church of England. Somehow the upshot of that decidedly contradictory combination was that I was raised with no religious training, and as a member of no particular faith. If anything, Protestant—but, if so, then nominally and nonpracticing. When I did come to reading and studying the Bible as an adult, its contradictions were what most fascinated, and it was to the Psalms that I found myself most often returning.

Of course, contradiction abounds throughout the Old Testament and is most often traceable back to God and the actions by which he manifests himself. The chief contradiction, it turns out, is not within God but between God and humankind, and the contradiction has entirely to do with what distinguishes one from the other, namely, mortality or the lack of it. To be mortal is to be vulnerable: Weakness or flexibility, by whichever name, is inherent to human nature. But God, though capable of creating weakness and giving it human shape, is apparently incapable of understanding it. If God is all-knowing, then I believe his knowing must be limited to the intellectual kind. Sensual knowledge is presumably not possible without flesh, which is vulnerable. Nor is it possible to understand—except, again, intellectually—the gestures that spring from such aspects of vulnerability as sorrow, regret, longing, and sorts of things that figure, for example, into the choice of Lot's wife to look back at the home she is leaving, despite God's command that she not do so. To the inflexibility of perfection, such gestures can only translate into defiance—hence the punishment the wife receives, for no reason that seems *humanly* logical. This is the only limitation I can find to being not only the dispenser of divine law, but the divine law itself. It makes sense that the God of the Old Testament is merciless; from his perspective, what can mercy be?

A fair number of the psalms are psalms of praise, of thanksgiving to God, for his having spared the speaker—for having been merciful and responsive, that is, to the speaker's hopes or prayers. But this gratitude seems to me misguided. What seems constant in the Old Testament is the fact of a divine plan or pattern, inscrutable to the limited vision of humans, but in place all the same. And those who do not conform or assist that plan will not be spared. This is the mercilessness of efficiency, bracing, not random at all, and perfect.

Psalms is arguably the most human book of the Old Testament because the psalms spring entirely from a human inability to accept the possibility of God as merciless and responsive only to a will or plan of his own. Prayer may be one-directional on the surface—audible prayer does not tend to receive audible answer—but it has been human to want to believe that prayer elicits a response, in some form. If George Herbert likens prayer—in his poem by the same name—to "a reversèd thunder," he also ends the poem by equating prayer with "something understood," that is, understood by another, the listener presumably, whom he would believe God to be. If our belief in response is willed and desperate, it is desperation; if confident, we call it faith. Both occur in the Psalms, testifying to the book's necessary contradictions. For every psalm of praise, there seems as well a psalm of railing despair, rising from the human inability to understand God's ways. To put it more bluntly, the psalmist praises God when things go well, and doesn't when they don't. True faith, as I understand it, has little room for this sort of inconstancy, any more than perfection—given its inflexibility—has room for bargaining.

And yet a sense of bargaining or wager is everywhere in the Psalms; and again, I would say this too is uniquely human, because to bargain is to assume persuadability or flexibility: human characteristics, not divine ones. It's an example of what Xenophanes famously noted: that divinity will always be conceived of in terms consistent with the character and traits of the believer. Hence the opening line of Psalm 30:

> I will extol thee, O Lord; *for* thou has lifted me up, and hast not made my foes to rejoice over me.

Or, from 51:

> Cast me not away from thy presence; and take not thy Holy Spirit from me.
> Restore unto me the joy of thy salvation; and uphold me with thy free Spirit.
> *Then* will I teach transgressors thy ways; and sinners shall be converted unto thee.
> Deliver me from bloodguiltiness, O God, thou God of my salvation; *and* my tongue shall sing aloud of thy righteousness.

And again, from 116:

> I love the Lord, *because* he hath heard my voice and my supplication.
> *Because* he hath inclined his ear unto me, *therefore* will I call upon him as long as I live.

The words I've italicized above are surely from the syntax of bargain, of consequence, of conditions put forth and variously met, unmet, or in the balance. Perhaps, among the empirically minded, faith can only be conditional. We require proof, or at the least we have an instinct toward proof. I'm willing to say that bargaining is not the only word for what's at work in the psalms I've cited: Psalm 30 is also an articulation of thanksgiving, an *ex-voto*; 51 is a lovely example of repentance, of a willingness to atone; and perhaps 116 can be seen as an instance of spiritual awakening, of recognition and consequent action in accord with a new appreciation for God's gifts. Nevertheless, to my mind these are all versions of bargain, testimonials to a call having won or still hoping to win a response.

As the psalms of praise in the face of suffering are written in the immediate wake of having received the requested answer to a cry for help, so are the psalms of bewilderment or despair written in the wake of the *withholding* of deliverance. They carry the sensibility of one who feels she has upheld her part of the agreement, while God has failed to uphold his. In Psalm 22, the psalmist falls back on an ancestral history of a fair relationship between God and humankind, and this is put forward as a way of showing how God has faltered in terms of reliability:

> My God, my God, why hast thou forsaken me? why are thou so far from
>   helping me, and from the words of my roaring?
> Oh my God, I cry in the daytime, but thou hearest not; and in the night
>   season, and am not silent.
> But thou art holy, O thou that inhabitest the praises of Israel.
> Our fathers trusted in thee: they trusted, and thou didst deliver them.
> They carried unto thee, and were delivered: they trusted in thee, and were
>   not confounded. (1–5)

In Psalm 44, the history is not ancestral but more immediately personal. And the tone is decidedly more accusatory, beginning with a list of sufferings directly attributed to God, then moving on to a record of how devoted the sufferers have always been—therefore undeserving of such suffering—and turning finally from there to questions that, by implication, demand of God some explanation:

> Thou has given us like sheep appointed for meat; and hast scattered us
>   among the heathen.
> Thou sellest thy people for nought, and dost not increase thy wealth by
>   their price.

Thou makest us a reproach to our neighbors, a scorn and a derision to
   them that are round about us.
Thou makest us a byword among the heathen, a shaking of the head
   among the people.
My confusion is continually before me, and the shame of my face hath
   covered me,
For the voice of him that reproacheth and blasphemeth; by reason of the
   enemy and avenger.
All this is come upon us; yet have we not forgotten thee, neither have we
   dealt falsely in thy covenant.
Our heart is not turned back, neither have our steps declined from
   thy way;
Though thou hast sore broken us in the place of dragons, and covered us
   with the shadow of death.
If we have forgotten the name of our God, or stretched out our hands to a
   strange god;
Shall not God search this out? for he knoweth the secrets of the heart.
Yea, for thy sake are we killed all the day long; we are counted as sheep for
   the slaughter.
Awake, why sleepest thou, O Lord? arise, cast us not off for ever.
Wherefore hidest thou thy face, and forgettest our affliction and our
   oppression? (11–24)

Is this faith, on the part of the psalmist? If so, it's a qualified one, to
be sure—not unswerving; conflicted. But I begin to think that that's
one of the (no doubt unintentional) effects of the Psalms when read
as a whole: they serve as nothing less than an honest record of human
faith, complete with its flaws, its tendency to sway and buckle, to yield
as easily to fear and anger as (when things go well) to joy, praise, and
appreciation. I call the record honest, because it seems to me that this
muddled kind of faith is the only kind of which a vulnerable, flawed
creature such as a human being is capable.

   And perhaps faith, finally, is in the utterance alone. Whether bar-
gaining with, praising, or railing against, the majority of the psalms are
utterances directed *toward*—which is to say that even to utter is to show
a belief in a listener or to show a *desire* to believe in such a listener. Many
of the psalms speak to or about a God who is said to have hidden or
have turned away; nowhere does the psalmist doubt that God exists.

This is human faith, as I see it, one that argues that a belief in God need not mean an unshakeable allegiance to and acceptance of all of the *ways* of God. Humans are distinguishable from other animals by self-consciousness—by ego. And it is ego that makes humans the only creatures capable of articulating a felt worship of God; it is also ego, however, that makes a robotic allegiance to God impossible. Presumably, God knows this, as he knows his presence could not be fully understood without, occasionally, his seeming absence.

An untested faith isn't worth that much, it seems to me. And an untested God? Again I turn to Herbert, who in his poem "Artillery" suggests that God is subject to the laws he has fashioned for his creatures:

> My tears and prayers night and day do woo,
> And work up to thee; yet thou dost refuse.
> > Not but I am (I must say still)
> > Much more obliged to do thy will,
> > Than thou to grant mine: but because
> Thy promise now hath ev'n set thee thy laws.
>
> Then we are shooters both, and thou dost deign
> To enter combat with us, and contest
> With thine own clay. (19–27)[1]

We are bargaining, again—yes?

◆ ◆ ◆

The trajectory—psychological, emotional—of the Psalms is that of restiveness itself. It is true that the book as a whole ends with an uncharacteristically sustained note of joyful praise (from Psalm 145 through 150, the last). But crescendo isn't always conclusion; and if we have read the entire book, we cannot help but understand that the only constant here is fluctuation, the ease with which astonishment gives way to joy, joy to fear, fear to despair, and despair again—and temporarily—to joy. This is the restiveness of what it is to be human and perishable. To be flawed. To be alive.

Maybe an absolutely unqualified, unquestioned belief in deity is like those limits in calculus, the point that a line approaches infinitely without intersection, though theoretically intersection must eventually occur. Call belief the point of intersection, call the ever-approaching line the will to believe. Say the point of intersection is shared by God *and* belief—that is, belief in God occurs *at* God, and vice versa. And the ever-approaching line that we are calling the will to believe? Say another word for that is faith.

✦   ✦   ✦

What the soul apparently wants of the body is the perfection of absolute obedience. But the body comes equipped with instinct; and instinct, more than having a will of its own, *is* that will. Is devotion the same as obedience? Must it mean utterly giving oneself up to another power? What is the difference between apprenticeship and thralldom, except the degree of submission? How far is folly?

In Virgil's *Aeneid*, Dido—the queen of Carthage—has made a vow of chastity, a devotion to the memory of her dead husband Sychaeus. Soon after the arrival, of the hero Aeneas, however, Dido realizes that she has fallen in love with Aeneas, and she recognizes the conflict between what she has promised the dead and what she feels toward the living. It's a conflict between *types* of devotion. Dido consults with her sister, who encourages Dido to enjoy life—and love—while she can. But the world—or perhaps only Virgil's notions of it?—was more rigid back then: a vow was a vow, and to break it was sacrilege, and it is disappointing but not surprising as we watch Dido swiftly descend the steps of the doom awaiting her, in the form of death by self-immolation on a burning pyre.

But the contemporary world—or perhaps this is only my own notion of it—is one of flexible morality, for better *and* worse. Devotion to the dead, to the living, to a deity, or to a desire to believe that there *is* anything like deity: why do we have to choose? What is so unreasonable about thinking of devotion as many-faceted, multidimensional? That trajectory of restiveness graphed out across the Psalms: if the restiveness of being human, why not also the restiveness of devotion? Why not say that there are to devotion, as to being human, many parts, and necessarily they won't be absolutely reconciled in this life?

These weren't questions that occurred to me when I first read about Dido in my senior year of high school. But about twenty-five years later, I did think about such questions while I was visiting Herring Cove Beach in Provincetown, Massachusetts. Typically, for high summer, the beach was packed. I had settled for the day on that part of the beach which, by some unwritten, unspoken law, has always been occupied primarily by gay men. Here and there, I'd see a man lying on a large beach towel beside a small pile or ring of stones—as if the stones were sharing the man's towel. It turned out that these were meant as cairns of a sort, tangible representations of a partner, friend, or lover who had died. In effect, the men were spending the day at the beach—the beach the two of them had often enjoyed together—with the dead, with the (concretized) *memory* of the dead.

What was devotion, if not this?

But the more closely I observed these men, the more I realized that devotion had not meant a diminishment in sexual desire. Each man was keenly aware of the others around him, and the charge in the air was decidedly sexual. If not actually cruising, the men were certainly not indifferent to the *possibility* of sex—there was at the least an openness to it.

And it seemed to me then that sexual attraction to the living need not compromise our devotion to the memory of the dead. Perhaps—even more dangerously—sexual attraction need not compromise our devotion to the living, either. These men did not seem undevoted; rather, they seemed what some might call divided in their loyalties. For me, they were granting devotion—like morality more broadly—a flexibility without which how can we begin to call ourselves human beings, which is to say not perfect, only perfectly human?

◆ ◆ ◆

In so many books of the Old Testament, we find a prescription for correct human behavior, or narratives that seem to conceal such a prescription. The Psalms provide us with the enactment of all types of human behavior, and there is none of the reconciliation that attends prescription—no easy "if X, then Y" mathematics. That is, the Psalms allow us to believe in *ourselves*, in the many parts of which we are made, including that part that would like to believe there is something more, finally, than just ourselves.

For some of us, one of the larger parts is the one that would like to make art; or more exactly, the part that makes what it would like to believe is art—and perhaps even have others believe, as well. I began this essay by speaking of art and the making of it because I see a parallel between the contradictions that the artist is drawn to, contains, enacts, and those contradictions that make up the sensibility of the Psalms. The sensibility of the Psalms is, finally, an artistic one—which should not surprise: the psalmist was, after all, an artist.

Another way to read the Psalms is as a graphing of that trajectory of restiveness which belongs particularly to the artist. Like God, art is not quantifiable—publications, exhibits, reviews notwithstanding, it is impossible to define precisely what art is; or, if art, whether good or bad art. The ultimate subjectivity of art makes it as distant and abstract as God, and I would equate the urge to make art with spiritual faith: we believe, or want to, that somewhere there is the equivalent of answered prayer, of divine attention; we call it audience—something that, even if we aren't conscious of it during the act of creation, we must somewhere have in mind. When I write a poem, it's because I have something I need to say, and wish to; and it seems only reasonable that to say something is to believe in someone or something to say it to. Utterance, again, as a form of faith.

Among the many things feared by the psalmist, two stand out. One is the fear of becoming "a reproach of men," in particular for having had faith at all:

> All they that see me laugh me to scorn: they shoot out the lip, they shake
> the head, saying,
> He trusted in the Lord that he would deliver him: let him deliver him,
> seeing he delighted in him. (22:7–8)

But the fear is broader than that. The psalmist fears reproach of many kinds: sometimes the shame of defeat,

> O my God, I trust in thee: let me not be ashamed, let not mine enemies
> triumph over me. (25:2)

sometimes mockery,

> But in mine adversity they rejoiced. . . . They did tear me, and ceased not:
> With hypocritical mockers in feasts, they gnashed upon me with their
> teeth. (35:15–16)

> Let them be desolate for a reward of their shame that say unto me, Aha,
> aha. (40:15)

and sometimes slander,

> For the mouth of the wicked and the mouth of the deceitful are opened
> against me: they have spoken against me with a lying tongue.
> They compassed me about also with words of hatred; and fought against
> me without a cause. (109:2–3)

The other fear often expressed in the Psalms is of abandonment by
God:

> But mine eyes are unto thee, O God the Lord: in thee is my trust; leave
> not my soul destitute. (144:8)

> Lord, why castest thou off my soul? why hidest thou thy face from me?
> (88:14)

> Why withdrawest thou thy hand, even thy right hand? (74:11)

> O God, thou hast cast us off, thou hast scattered us, thou hast been
> displeased; O turn thyself to us again. (60:1)

What are artists most bedeviled by? On one hand, the fear that
a belief in the art they make will turn out to have been a misplaced
one—hence, the anxiety that surrounds the art, once it's put out into
the world: what will the reaction be? Mockery? Hatred?

Another fear: the fear of abandonment, in the form of indifference,
not only from the audience but—worse—from no less a force than the
Muse herself, analogous to God, for artists. What if there is nothing
else forthcoming? What if she who brought us here should turn her
face? One of the shrewder instances of this particular anxiety occurs

at the end of "The Wish," a poem from Louise Glück's *Meadowlands*. Estranged husband and wife have each made a separate wish. He imagines that what she wished for was for him to return to her, and for the two of them to be together again. Her response:

> I wished for what I always wish for.
> I wished for another poem. (9–10)[2]

In an interview for *Callaloo*, editor Charles Rowell asked me to speak a bit about the title of my third book, *From the Devotions*. My response:

> [T]he poems come out of, as it were, a book of devotions, in that medieval sense, where daily one would reflect on one's faith in one way or another, as a means of coming closer to the deity—or, in terms of my book, to whatever is true for each person. It's not a religious book by any means—but it's an intensely spiritual one, which is a very different thing from being religious. And what more spiritual acts are there than loving somebody, or than writing, itself? These acts are just as much an attempt to approach what is ever-elusive, as in prayer. I think of writing as prayer. And sex is also prayer.

ANTHEM

Trapped bee at the glass.

A window.

Instinct is different from
to *understand*.

Is not the same.

The window is not the light
it fills with—has
been filling with—

What the bee ascends to.

Is full with.

To ascend.
To have been foiled.
To be consistent.

Instinct making
its own equations.

The window is not, for the bee, a window.

Is a form of resistance.

not understood
because not understandable,
not in terms

of reason
A felt force.

A force entirely:

And I said Yes. That it
had been

like that. Resistance
equaling,
at first, the light—And then resistance

as only one of the light's more difficult

and defining features.

If I call it a psalm, is it?

◆   ◆   ◆

—Isn't it?

NOTES

1. George Herbert, "Artillery," in *The English Poems of George Herbert*, ed.
Helen Wilcox (Cambridge: Cambridge University Press, 2007), 484.
2. Louise Glück, "The Wish," in *Meadowlands* (New York: Ecco Press, 1997).

PSALM AND ANTI-PSALM

A Personal Interlude

Alicia Ostriker

> I hate and love. Why, you perhaps might ask.
> I don't know. But I feel it, and it is excruciating.
> —Catullus

A few days after the destruction of the World Trade Center in New York City on September 11, 2001, the recently inaugurated poet laureate of the United States, Billy Collins, was interviewed by the journalist Sandra Martin. Asked what role poetry might play at such a moment, he replied that for him poetry was a private art and needed a private focus. In a public radio interview on September 11 itself, he suggested that almost any page of any book of poetry would be "speaking for life . . . against what happened today." Or, he said, read the Psalms.[1]

The Psalms? Was he joking?

The Psalms are glorious. No, the Psalms are terrible. No, the Psalms are both glorious and terrible, both attractive and repulsive emotionally and theologically. I read as a poet and a woman, a literary critic and a left-wing Jew who happens to be obsessed with the Bible. And when I read these poems, I experience a split-screen effect: wildly contradictory responses.

To adapt Catullus: I love and hate.

A JOYFUL NOISE

The Psalms are overwhelmingly beautiful as poems. They represent the human spirit, my own spirit, in its intimate yearning for a connection with the divine Being who is the source of all being, the energy that creates and sustains the universe. Unlike the portions of the Bible that lay down rules and regulations, and unlike the narratives that tell compelling tales of patriarchs and matriarchs, judges, warriors and kings, but do not tell how they feel, what they think, what it all means to them—the Psalms are love poems to God. Since the course of true love never does run smooth, the Psalms are poems of emotional turbulence.

Sometimes the psalmist expresses a wonderfully serene, almost childlike faith and trust. "The Lord is my shepherd; I shall not want. He makes me to lie down in green pastures. He leads me beside the still waters. He restores my soul." The ineffable sweetness of this pastoral image surely taps a deep human desire to be relieved of responsibility, including the responsibility of being human. Is that why the Twenty-third Psalm is the most popular in the whole psalter? In "He restores my soul," the Hebrew for "my soul" is *nafshi*, a term humans share with animals. It is wonderful, too, that the psalmist does not declare "I am a sheep" or "I am like a sheep," but speaks directly as from the animal soul, the *nefesh*, itself. In Psalm 37 we are advised not to "fret" over evildoers; they are going to disappear, and "the meek shall inherit the earth." All of us who are meek, who feel powerless on earth, can identify with this fantasy. Sometimes a psalm runs a video in my frontal lobe, and causes my back to straighten and my lungs to pull in air—"I will lift up my eyes unto the hills, whence cometh my help. My help cometh from the Lord, who made heaven and earth" (121:1–2). These two sentences are so physical, but then so metaphysical, shaped like a chiasmus (a kind of word sandwich) but also striking a sequence of registers that expand into larger and larger space: body (eyes), natural environment (vista of hills), cosmos (heaven, earth). I catch my breath every time. I feel confident and alive every time. Commercials for recreational vehicles profiled against a mountain sunrise try to press the same button of exhilaration in me, but something is missing. Commercial culture gives me nothing like this:

> My help cometh from the Lord, who made heaven and earth. He will not suffer thy foot to be moved. He that keepeth thee will not slumber . . . The Lord is thy keeper. The Lord is thy shade upon thy right hand. The sun shall not smite thee by day nor the moon by night. The Lord shall preserve thee from all evil.

God is connected to nature, as its maker. God is in the hills, God is in the mountains. God made heaven and earth, so you and I are protected by the entire cosmos, which makes us quite safe. God even makes it possible to shift pronouns from me to you without a touch of anxiety. And look at the security blanket of language when the psalmist has "behaved and quieted myself, like a child just weaned from his mother. My soul is like a weaned child" (131:2). Not a child in the womb or a nursing child, but one who has left those comforts behind, and probably wept for them, but is still confident of being loved.

At other moments the psalmist is racked by doubt and self-doubt. "How long wilt thou forget me, O Lord? Forever?" (13:1). Here is a voice of suffering, complaining, crying out, feeling abandoned, hurt, tormented. "My God, my God, why have you forsaken me? Why art thou so far from helping me, and from the mouth of my roaring?" (22:1). It seems evident that wicked people prosper in this world, that good people suffer, and that God refuses to intervene. "Why standest thou far off, O Lord? Why hidest thou in time of trouble? The wicked persecute the poor. . . . [The wicked man] boasts of his heart's desire. . . . As for his enemies, he puffeth at them" (10:1–3, 5). Or, as we would say, the bad guy blows off anyone who bothers him. "They are enclosed in their own fat, with their mouths they speak proudly" (17:10). "And they say, How does God know?" (73:11). "O God, how long shall the adversary reproach? Shall the enemy blaspheme thy name for ever?" (74:10). Evildoers get away with murder, they are shameless, and the psalmist passionately begs God to help.

Many psalms evoke experiences of being alone, attacked, persecuted, punished. Some beg forgiveness for sin: "Have mercy upon me, O God. . . . A broken spirit and a contrite heart, O God, thou wilt not despise" (51:1, 17). Many speak from desperation. "Save me, O God, for the waters have come into my soul. I sink in deep mire. The ones that hate me without a cause are more than the hairs of my head" (69:1–4). "My days are consumed like smoke. My heart is withered like grass" (102:3–4). I recognize the sense of sinking dread, the feeling that my life is meaningless, that my emotions have dried up. The poetry articulates my dread and dryness in exquisite figurative language, which makes it hurt both less, because of the beauty, and more, because of the accuracy. And then the feeling modulates with incredible subtlety. One of my favorite psalms is 42: "As the hart pants after the water brooks, so my soul pants after thee, O God" (42:1). What a melancholy yet sweet image of the desire for God, the desire of a thirsting animal. The soul, my soul, is *nafshi* again, here. The yearning is as pure as that physical need. But then it turns. "My soul thirsts for God, for the living God. When shall I come and appear before God? My tears have been my meat night and day while they continually say unto me, 'where is thy God?'" (42: 2–3). It is not simply that I fruitlessly long to be close to God, united with God, but that at the same time, and precisely because everyone knows I go around with this spiritual need, people mock me. Those who do not have my faith or my need, and do not want it, and can live their lives nicely without it, mock me. Evidently it gives them satisfaction to ridicule me. And let me remember that men and women for eons have been mocked in far worse circumstances than mine: in jail, under interrogation, under torture, at the point of martyrdom. I imagine there was considerable mockery, and self-mockery, in the concentration camps of Europe in the last century.

Then again many psalms express jubilation, celebration, wonder, awe. "Make a joyful noise unto God, all ye lands" (66:1) is a tone repeatedly struck. "Sing unto God a new song" (96:1), with the sense that God is present throughout the cosmos, and everywhere at once awesome and delightful. "Let everything that lives and breathes give praise to the Lord" (150:6). The Hebrew title for the book of Psalms is *Tehillim*, derived from *hallel*, "to praise" (source of the word "hallelujah"), and means "Praises":

> Whither shall I go from thy spirit, or whither shall I flee from thy
> presence? If I send up into heaven, thou art there. If I make my bed
> in hell, behold, thou art there. If I take the wings of the morning and
> dwell in the uttermost parts of the sea, even there shall thy hand lead
> me and thy right hand hold me. (139:7–10)

This begins with an edge of fear, the suggestion of a wish to escape, but turns out to be very close to love-play, love-teasing, especially in its echo of the sensuousness of the Song of Songs: "His right hand is under my head, and his left hand embraces me." The voice of the psalmist is the voice of one who would like to be experiencing this sublime wonder, this intimacy, this sense of being surrounded by a tenderly loving yet cosmically powerful God, day and night. Of course it doesn't happen that way, just as in our own relationships. The emotions of the Psalms surge and collapse like breaking waves, as they do in our own emotional lives. There is joy and despair and hope and frustration and fear and anger and grief and sorrow, and then the desperation breaks like a wave into trust and joy again.

Uncontrollable, unpredictable. Scholars have tried in vain to find an orderly structure in the sequence of psalms, since they contain very little in the way of rhyme or reason to them. They are not rational; they are intense. Anyone who meditates knows how unruly the mind is. You try to still it and make it serene, and it fails to obey. This is what we find in the Psalms too. They are like a magnifying glass that seems to be looking at the presence and withdrawal of God, but in another sense can be said to be looking at the capacity of the mind to secrete its own calm—and then its inability to grasp that calm for more than moments at a time. What does remain constant throughout is faith that God exists, whether present or absent. "The fool says in his heart that there is no God" (14:1), but in the world of the Psalms, only a fool would think such a thing. In the world of the Psalms, God is ultimately our deliverer; we have only to trust. "They that sow in tears shall reap in joy" (126:5).

All this makes for magnificent poetry, obviously—the kind that survives translation in language, time, and space. The Psalms exist in hundreds of languages and form an endless source for Jewish, Christian, and Muslim culture. The idea of faith, love, and devotion in the Psalms saturates the Gospels, whose early readers would of course have known the Psalms well, since they form a central part of Jewish liturgy. When Jesus in the beatitudes says that the meek shall inherit the earth, he repeats the psalmist's wishful thinking. When he declares, "If any one thirst, let him come to me and drink," he takes the trope of spiritual thirst from Psalm 42. When on the cross he cries, "My God, my God, why hast thou forsaken me," he is crying out as a Jew in his death as well as in his life.

The Psalms have inspired mystics through the centuries, and continue to inspire poets beyond the boundaries of conventional religion. Think, for example, of Whitman's insistence on celebrating every jot and tittle of the created world. Or the close of W. H. Auden's elegy on W. B. Yeats, with its parallel death-and-rebirth motif:

> Follow, poet, follow right
> To the bottom of the night
> . . . .
> With your uncomplaining voice
> Still persuade us to rejoice
> . . . .
> In the prison of his days
> Teach the free man how to praise.

How to praise is one great lesson of the Psalms. Literature in English is irrigated by these poems not only because of the multitude of memorable phrases in the King James Version that I and other poets steal, but also because they are always telling us to celebrate, praise, open ourselves to the universe. That is the task of the poet, or at least I take it to be my task as a poet and a human being, to open myself in praise of an existence that inevitably includes suffering, anguish, pain, despair.

A poem by Sharon Olds typifies the way the Psalms can be used in ways that may seem shocking but are perfectly faithful to their spirit. The poem is called "Sex without Love" and is an attempt to imagine how they "do it," the people who make love without love:

> How do they come to the
> come to the   come to the   God   come to the
> still waters and not love
> the one that came there with them.

Lifted directly from the Twenty-third Psalm, the poem's stumbling incredulity assumes that when we do love the person we make love with, it is like that moment of blissful safety in the Psalms where we know ourselves to be cared for by the Lord who is our shepherd.

A ROD OF IRON

Magnificent poems. When I read them through the lens of politics, I shudder at their magnificence. It is perhaps a figure-and-ground problem. Let me point out that although there has been an explosion of scholarly and critical writing about the Bible by women in the last fifteen or twenty years, almost nothing has been written about the book of Psalms by contemporary women scholars. That is rather curious. Part of the reason, surely, is that unlike books of the Bible such as Genesis, Exodus, the Song of Songs, the book of Ruth, or the Scroll of Esther, or even Proverbs, with its stereotyped portraits of the evil seductress and the good woman whose price is above rubies, Psalms contains no women at all. No Eve with her talking snake and her fruit, no laughter of Sarah, no Miriam with her timbrels and her song.

But the problem runs deeper. We do not take literally the old idea that the Psalms were composed by King David, yet the psalmist often seems less a generic human than a public man. A politician, a warrior. In the Psalms the sun may rise like a bridegroom running to meet his bride, but nothing like domestic life or domestic imagery enters. What I hear—when I read consciously as a woman with antiwar leanings—are the personal meditations and intimate feelings of a man who feels himself to be surrounded by enemies. Are his enemies personal rivals? Are they political or military foes? The categories seem virtually interchangeable. An enemy is an enemy. The psalmist's enemies are *evildoers*, *workers of iniquity*, and *adversaries*. They are *the proud* and *the heathen*. They *blaspheme* and are *violent*. They oppress the poor and the fatherless. And then again they *persecute* and *lay snares for* the psalmist.

How are we to interpret this motif? If the psalmist is David, the enemies might include King Saul, who through much of I Samuel is trying to hunt David down and kill him. Or the enemies might be the Philistines, against whom David waged many battles. But what about us, the readers? Insofar as you and I identify with these poems, our most dangerous and hurtful enemy is probably a family member, a neighbor, a co-worker, a boss. Perhaps an unspoken reason for the universal appeal of the Psalms is that ordinary people all over the world feel themselves to be at the mercy of enemies large and small. But here is the rub: In our lives, and the life of history, the animus against personal foes is made to accrue to public ones; the purpose of state propaganda is to take our personal frustration and anger and redirect them against the foes of our rulers. We the people can always be manipulated to hate some demonized Other. At the same time, whatever damage we endure at the hands of those more powerful than ourselves can be taken out on whoever is weaker than ourselves. "Those to whom evil is done / Do evil in return," as Auden points out in "September 1, 1939," the poem most widely circulated in the wake of the World Trade Center attack. The interchangeability of public and private hostilities is finely mirrored by the ambiguities of the Psalms.

Fascinatingly, in this world of mighty rhetoric, the sins are commonly sins of the tongue. "His mouth is full of cursing and deceit and fraud" (10:7); they "have sharpened their tongues like a serpent" (140:3); their "mouth speaketh vanity" (144:8). They are foes of Israel, foes of God, and the psalmist wants them destroyed. Is it yearning for goodness and justice on earth that drives his fantasies, is it yearning for vengeance, is it mere hatred of Otherness? Can we necessarily tell the difference? An enemy is an enemy. Occasionally the imagery of punishment is less than lethal, but it is always urgently physical. "Thou shalt break them with a rod of iron; thou shalt dash them in pieces like a potter's vessel" (2:9). "Break thou the arm of the wicked and the evil man" (10:15). "Upon the wicked shall he rain snares, fire and brimstone" (11:6). "The enemies of the Lord shall be as the fat of lambs: they shall consume; into smoke they shall consume away" (37:20). "Break their teeth, O God, in their mouth: break out the great teeth of the young lions, O Lord. Let them melt away like water. . . . The righteous shall rejoice when he seeth the vengeance: he shall wash his feet in the blood of the wicked" (58:6–7, 10). Magnificent poetry. Sublimated aggression (which, like latent energy, is easily converted to action). State propaganda. Psychological projection. All of the above. All.

Part of what makes the dream of punishing the enemy in the Psalms so forceful is the way punishment blooms like a flower from pathos. Poetically, the "turn" of numerous psalms is from devastating grief to its redress, which is sometimes an expectation of deliverance in generalized terms and sometimes the more exciting promise that our enemies will be destroyed. Psalm 137, one of the most evocative in the psalter, speaks from the perspective of the Israelites driven into exile and slavery after the Babylonian destruction of Jerusalem in 587 B.C.E. In a way it is a typical psalm, full of unpredictable changes in tone. It begins with a picture of a crowd of people carrying their few belongings sitting by a river that is not their home.

> By the waters of Babylon, there we sat down, yea, we wept when we
> remembered Zion. We hanged our harps upon the willows in the
> midst thereof. For there they that carried us away captive required of
> us a song; and they that wasted us required of us mirth, saying, Sing us
> one of the songs of Zion.

These extraordinary opening lines, which audiences all over the world today know from Bob Marley's reggae version, convey a scene of conventional beauty—a river with its willows—suffused by a collective sorrow. The sitting down on the ground is extended by tears falling and harps hanging, further images of helplessness. Simultaneously, the sitting and the hanging up of harps is also a kind of passive disobedience during a forced march. And is there not a relation between the waters of Babylon and the flowing tears? Then the mood shifts from simple grief to irony. The bitterness of being mocked by those who are stronger, which is such a powerful theme throughout Psalms, is particularly piercing here. "How can we sing the Lord's song in a strange land?" Nothing in poetry so succinctly captures the trauma of exile. Our enemies, who have conquered our land, have destroyed our homes and our holy temple, and are herding us along, are making fun of us by asking us to sing, in effect, a psalm. The demand is not only cruel but also absurd. How can we sing God's song in a foreign land? The Hebrew Bible claims throughout that the children of Israel cannot separate their identity as a people from the land God has given them. This portion of Psalm 137 is like saying, "We not only won't sing; we can't. Song cannot come out of us if we are not in our homeplace."

And then comes the moment of the vow. I may be in exile now, but I will never forget. These next lines at once intensify and reverse the grief at captivity: "If I forget thee, O Jerusalem, may my right hand forget her cunning. May my tongue cleave to the roof of my mouth if I remember not Jerusalem above my chief joy." Notice the shift from first-person plural "we" to the singular "I," and how the hand that acts, and the tongue that converses and sings, become subject to the mind that swears not to become assimilated to the alien culture. I do everything with my right hand, so these lines are asking to be paralyzed if I fail to cherish the memory of Jerusalem above every other pleasure in my life. And in fact the passion of the exile for the homeland has remained alive in Judaism for two thousand years since the destruction of the second temple in the year 70 of the common era. Jews in diaspora ritually promise each other "next year in Jerusalem" at the close of every year's Passover feast.

The poignance of the vow in Psalm 137 is extraordinary. It signals a spiritual triumph over the initial scene of powerlessness, as if declaring that Babylon may capture bodies but not souls. At this point the psalmist turns to God, reminding God of the destruction of his own sacred city: "Remember, O Lord, the children of Edom in the day of Jerusalem; who said, Raze it, raze it, even to the foundation thereof." And finally comes the poem's prophetic conclusion: "O daughter of Babylon, who art to be destroyed, happy shall he be, that rewardeth thee as thou hast served us. Happy shall he be, that taketh and dasheth thy little ones against the stones."

And there we have it, human history, the justification of every blood feud, every literal dashing of children's heads against walls by conquering armies, guerrilla armies, occupying forces, terrorist suicide bombers, Arab and Jew, Serb and Bosnian, Hutu and Tutsi, Irish Protestants and Irish Catholics, Buddhist and Hindu in Sri Lanka, Hindu and Muslim throughout the Indian subcontinent, the Shining Path in Peru, to name a few current instances. Not to mention the Crusades, the Inquisition, the burning of heretics at the stake, the religious wars of the sixteenth and

seventeenth centuries in England and Europe, the pogroms, the Holo-
caust. The righteous, with God on their side, joyously washing their feet
in the blood of the wicked. The righteous, confident that they, and they
alone, know God's wishes, and are the only ones pure enough to carry
out God's will. Osama Bin Laden, shortly after the attack that destroyed
the World Trade Center, issued a statement broadcast throughout the
Islamic world. Isn't the rhetoric chillingly familiar?

> Praise be to God and we beseech Him for help and
> Forgiveness. We seek refuge with the Lord . . . .
> He whom God guides is rightly guided but he whom God
> leaves to stray, for him wilt thou find no protector to
> lead him to the right way.
>
> I witness that there is no God but God and Mohammed
> is his slave and Prophet.
>
> God Almighty hit the United States at its most vulnerable
> spot. He destroyed its greatest buildings. Praise be to God.
> Here is the United States. It was filled with terror from its
> north to its south and from its east to its west. Praise be to God.
>
> They champion falsehood, support the butcher against the
> victim, the oppressor against the innocent child. May God
> mete them the punishment they deserve.[2]

A handwritten document left behind by a leader among the hijackers,
Mohammed Atta, urges the prospective hijacker/martyr: "You should
pray, you should fast. You should ask God for guidance. . . . Purify your
heart and clean it from all earthly matters." Among the prayers: "O God,
open all doors for me. O God, who answers prayers and answers those
who ask you, I am asking you for your help. . . . God, I trust in you. God,
I lay myself in your hands."[3]

The Psalms are the prototype in English of devotional poetry and
possibly of lyric poetry in general. Let nobody say that poetry makes
nothing happen. Let nobody say that poetry cannot or should not be
political. We have this model before us.

Jews, Christians, and Muslims, and pagans before us,[4] have worshipped
a God—have created a God to worship—who is both tender and violent.

God is father, judge, warrior, mighty arm, rock, redeemer, and (with a little help from his friends) destroyer of the godless, which in practice can mean anyone I take to be my enemy. Is there any way to get around this? A famous sermon by the German theologian Dietrich Bonhoeffer, written in 1937 on the brink of World War II, in which he died a martyr of the resistance to Hitler, tries to rescue Psalm 58, "this frightful psalm of vengeance," by claiming that it is not really we sinners who "are able to pray this psalm." Psalm 58 is the one in which the enemy's teeth are to be knocked out and the righteous are to wash their feet in the blood of the wicked. The speaker of the psalm, says Bonhoeffer, is King David—or, rather, Jesus Christ praying from within David, for "only he who is totally without sin can pray like that." We sinners must entrust vengeance to God, and endure suffering "without a thought of hate, and without protest." Moreover, if we shudder at the image of the righteous splashing about in the blood of the guilty, we must understand that the death sentence has already been enacted on Jesus, "the Savior who died for the godless, struck down by God's revenge," that the "bloodstained Savior" redeems whoever prostrates himself at the Cross. Jesus, then, is both the psalm's author and its victim; the true Christian is not responsible. Still, Bonhoeffer's solution perpetuates a familiar rhetoric of "the godless," as if we could be certain who they are, and supports a vehemently traditional view of God as chief officer of retribution.[5] In effect, Bonhoeffer recommends that good Christians avoid guilt and leave the punishing of sinners to God. It sounds, though I hesitate to say so, like Pilate washing his hands. In actuality, Bonhoeffer became involved in the conspiracy of German officers to assassinate Hitler and was hanged in the concentration camp at Flossenbürg on April 9, 1945, one of four members of his immediate family to die at the hands of the Nazi regime.

A beautiful essay by Kathleen Norris, "The Paradox of the Psalms,"[6] takes another approach toward their violence. Norris writes of what she learned during a year-long residence at a Benedictine convent, where the Psalms are the liturgical mainstay, sung or recited at morning, noon and evening prayer. Asking, "How in the world can we read . . . these angry and often violent poems from an ancient warrior culture, [that] seem overwhelmingly patriarchal, ill tempered, moralistic?" She answers that they reflect emotional reality—that the pain in them is essential for praise, that the Psalms are full of anger because "anger is one honest reaction to pain," that women who are trained to deny pain and anger—including Benedictine women—may find their expression healthy, and that "as one sister explained, the 'enemies' vilified in the cursing psalms are best seen as 'my own demons, not enemies out there.'"

Of Psalm 137, Norris points out that it has a special poignance for women who experience the journey from girlhood to an adulthood that demands prettiness and niceness as a journey to exile. It also "expresses the bitterness of colonized people everywhere. . . . The speaker could be one of today's refugees or exiles, an illegal alien working for far less than minimum wage, a slave laborer in China." The vision of brutal vengeance at its close, "O Babylon, . . . happy is he who repays you the ills you brought on us, happy is he who shall dash your children on the rock," should come as no surprise, she observes; it is "the fruit of human cruelty." She goes on to say that psalms such as this ask us to recognize our own capacity for vengeance and to see it as "a potentially deadly vice" that may be "so consuming that not even the innocent are spared." We should, Norris says, pray over it. Good. But do the vengeance fantasies in the Psalms ask to be read this way? Or is it not, rather, Norris's special temperament that prompts her to read them thus? Aren't the vengeance fantasies in fact endorsed in the poems' theological framework? Endorsed, that is, by God? And, incidentally, is vengeance morally acceptable if it punishes "the guilty," and reprehensible only if it strikes "the innocent"? If so, we return to the sticky question of how guilt and innocence are to be determined and the likelihood that "the guilty" and "my enemies" will be mysteriously identical.

We may twist on the hook as we will. Once we have bitten the bait of the Psalms we are in the power of a vision that mirrors our minds. The character of God in these splendid poems is also our projection, deny it as we may. We create God in our image and attribute holiness and power to him. Catherine Madsen in "Notes on God's Violence" advocates facing the possibility that the biblical God's character "alternates between tender care and ferocious brutality, between limitless creation and wholesale wreckage," not because the biblical God rewards nice people and punishes bad ones, but because "the violence of the universe [is] at every point congruent with its nurturance" and because "Hebrew monotheism sets up one source for good and evil, one responsible will from which they both derive."[7]

The God who speaks to Job out of the whirlwind, that explosion of sublime amoral creativity, is the God of the Psalms, but with the veil of righteousness removed. And can one love such a God? And if one refuses, does praise too dry up? On the other hand, if one denies God's violence, is that not a kind of blasphemy? Stephen Mitchell, the brilliant translator of the Book of Job, recognizes the Voice from the whirlwind as embodying "the clarity, the pitilessness, of nature and of all great art."[8] Mitchell rightly points out how closely this vision of Job resembles the magnificent and terrifying play of divine creation and destruction revealed to Arjuna at the climax of the *Bhagavad Gita*. He quotes Blake's *Marriage of Heaven and Hell*: "The roaring of lions, the howling of wolves, the raging of the stormy sea, and the destructive sword, are portions of eternity too great for the eye of man."[9] Yet I once walked into a bookstore in Berkeley at a moment when Mitchell was reading his versions of Psalms, and I was appalled to hear him omit the close of Psalm 137, letting the poem end with the image of Jerusalem as the exile's chief joy, not with the image of the Babylonian child's head being dashed against a rock. I thought, Has New Age sentimental niceness claimed another victim? Is he trying to convert the Psalms to Buddhism?[10] Is he trying to castrate God? Who does he think he is fooling?

Why does the poet laureate of America, after terrorism has destroyed the World Trade Center and several thousand human lives in New York City, claim that poetry is about personal and not political matters? And why on earth does he cite the Psalms as "against" acts of terror?

WRESTLING WITH DIVINITY

My poems wrestle with the need of God, the violence of God. I should rather say that I let these matters attack and wrestle with my poems.

In 1999 I am working on a manuscript provisionally entitled "The Space of This Dialogue," after a sentence of Paul Celan, "Only in the space of this dialogue does that which is addressed take form and gather around the I who is addressing it." The experience is not so much of writing as of receiving. The poems arrive intermittently, and I have undertaken not to tell them what to say. They often address God, not expecting a response. Early in the process I write down some lines and call them "psalm." They are more like an anti-psalm. They say this:

> I am not lyric any more
> I will not play the harp
> for your pleasure
>
> I will not make a joyful
> noise to you, neither
> will I lament
>
> for I know you drink
> lamentation, too,
> like wine
>
> so I dully repeat
> you hurt me
> I hate you
>
> I pull my eyes away from the hills
> I will not kill for you
> I will never love you again
>
> unless you ask me[11]

What I recognize in the poem is my resistance to a God who deals cruelly with us and demands our praise. What the final line tells me is that I want to stop resisting. Perhaps I am like one of those abused woman who keeps forgiving her abuser. You read about them. They phone the police, then hide their bruises and refuse to press charges. Another poem ventriloquizes a pious voice that could emerge from any of the monotheistic faiths, and concludes with a last line that is, alas, a vast understatement:

One of these days
oh one of these days
will be a festival and a judgment
and our enemies will be thrown
into the pit while we rejoice
and sing hymns

Some people actually think this way

Later in the manuscript, writing during the 1999 bombing of Kosovo in the former Yugoslavia—remembering that this war of Christian against Muslim is typical of religious wars through the ages, in which God is the gun with which we shoot our enemy—I ask God what he is thinking. The question precipitates a dialogue:

century *the spot of black paint*
in the gallon of white
makes it whiter

so the evil impulse
is part of you
for a reason

what reason

greater wilder holiness

. . . .

so perhaps you want us to understand
it throbs also in you
like leavening

you want us to love that about you
even if you pray that your attribute of mercy
may overcome your attribute of wrath

you want us always to love the evil also
the death-wish also
the bread of hate

because we are your image
confess you prize
the cruel theater of it

An ancient rabbinic story describes God praying in the ruins of the destroyed temple. For what, it is asked, does God pray? God prays that his attribute of mercy will overcome his attribute of justice; my poem slightly alters the story. More painfully, the unnamed responding voice makes a declaration I cannot deny. It brings me to my knees. It sickens me. I am very well aware that I, like just about everyone else I know, rubberneck at traffic accidents. I am outraged by—and avidly read about and discuss—the horrors of war, torture, the wickedness of Congress and the current administration, oil interests, anyone whose politics or moral principles deviate from my own. As Elizabeth Bishop says in her poem to Marianne Moore, "We can bravely deplore." And we all enjoy deploring, don't we? Later still, to my surprise, appear poems such as this, which is again entitled "Psalm":

> I endure impure periods
> when I cannot touch you
>
> or even look at you
> you are a storm I would be electrocuted
>
> by your approach then I feel some sort of angelic laughter
> like children behind a curtain
>
> come, I think
> you are at my fingertips my womb
>
> you are the wild driver of my vehicle
> the argument in my poem
>
> nothing between us
> only breath

Where did that come from? I cannot imagine. I feel myself to be an aperture through which the words arrive. Like the biblical psalms, mine seem to be love poems to God. But I cannot justify my love.

NOTES

1. National Public Radio News Special, 3 p.m. ET, September 11, 2001.
2. CNN, October 7, 2001.
3. *International Herald Tribune*, Saturday–Sunday, September 29–30, 2001, 1, 4.
4. Jonas C. Greenfield, "The Holy Bible and Canaanite Literature," in *The*

Literary Guide to the Bible, ed. Robert Alter and Frank Kermode (Cambridge, MA: Harvard University Press, 1987), 552. Greenfield quotes as one example of the kind of poetry from which our psalms sprang:

> Now, your enemy, O Ba'al
> now, you smite your enemy
> you strike your adversary;
> you will take your eternal kingdom
> your everlasting dominion.

5. Dietrich Bonhoeffer, "Vengeance and Deliverance," in *A Testament to Freedom: The Essential Writings of Dietrich Bonhoeffer,* ed. Geffrey B. Kelly and F. Burton Nelson (New York: Harper Collins, 1990), 293–98.

6. Kathleen Norris, "The Paradox of the Psalms," in *Out of the Garden: Women Writers on the Bible,* ed. Christina Bachmann and Celina Spiegel (New York: Ballantine, 1994), 221–33.

7. Catherine Madsen, "Notes on God's Violence," *CrossCurrents* 51.2 (Summer 2001): 229–56.

8. *The Book of Job,* translated and with an introduction by Stephen Mitchell (New York: HarperCollins, 1992), xxi.

9. Ibid., xiv.

10. If so, this would be a very New Age Buddhism. As my Buddhist friend Michael Venditozzi points out to me, "I know no Buddhist (and no sane interpretation of Buddhism) that would leave out the dashing of the child's head. Quite the opposite, actually."

11. The work in progress described here was published as *The Volcano Sequence* (Pittsburgh, PA: University of Pittsburgh Press, 2002).

LOVER, DARK AND DANGEROUS

Jill Alexander Essbaum

To be loved by only the happy and the harmless is no great thrill. Therefore, in the wild of the night I confess it, if only to the inner depths and their darkness: far in the wandering wild, the landscape of my heart—half-heavy, half-hopeless, all acres of it filled with the shrub and thicket of everything that such a heaving organ as this can be filled with (take your pick of things)— right and rigid in the middle of it all is a cherry tree. And I love cherries.

The tree is overgrown, her branches sagging and shady. But the fruit is always ripe. The fruit is always red and sweet. There is nothing in any direction for miles but that delicious tree. The sun glows like a hot and pink rocket in the sky above. The air is thick with cherry. We find each other there and only there. When He comes, I am waiting, breathless, throbbing, my blouse awry and my hair brambled like a crown of thorns, painful and enigmatic. He will find me to be an easy lay, girlish, quivering, and very, very hungry. And I give myself over to His hands, to His lips and their wisdom, to His hands again. I drink from His cup and I am filled. He smells like fire and His rough skin sweats. He is swash and buckle both. This is my King, my Master. And here and only here—his God hands all over every inch of my secret flesh—I am divined, found out, uncovered. And then I am consumed.

◆ ◆ ◆

I have no method in me to divorce my experience of God from the pleasures of the body. Or, conversely, the absence of such bodily pleasures, when the lover is gone, itself a unique kind of pleasing pain. And I don't know that I want to separate it out. I have tried (indeed I often try in the present tense) praying to a God whose otherworldly importance demands exactly the kind of distant reverence appropriate perhaps to an elderly head of state, a hands-off brand of worship, a pantomime of praise. It works, but poorly so, and only for a little while. *Lord, Lord*, I say, but like Marcel Marceau and the contorted exaggerations of his face as his hands draw nearer to himself, the invisible box around me grows steadily smaller, its walls coming as close as they can bear until I am trapped in a prison of my own invention, choking on incense and piety.

◆ ◆ ◆

He is tall, like a man grown from the mountains. But He has a wisdom in His flesh, a warm knowing, and a sadness like light bidden from the stars, wounded, and from very far away. An ensuing strength rises from it. His hands—their broad palms hot and insistent—hold a beautiful violence. It is true. My breath skips a little at the thought of it. He reaches to touch His fingertip to the bared plain below my clavicle. A pulsing skin, a heart underneath it. Will He think of me, often or fondly? He sees through me with His fingers. He taps above my heart with His thumb. Will He carve the initials of us into the trunk of this witnessing tree? The cherry seems to groan for it. If we touch for much longer, He will know me. Nothing that is hidden will stay hidden. I am as anxious as only a waiting woman can be.

◆ ◆ ◆

The practice of my typically sterile devotions usually ends not with my gaining an audience with the Divine, but with an unceremonial giving up on my part. As if the sum efforts of my worship do not merit the small consolation they offer, I simply fall away. These times come and I spend my Sundays in bed. My Bible goes back into its cubbyhole on my aubergine-colored shelves, to collect its thoughts and its dust. God gets put on those ruddy shelves as well, the very idea of Him being too much for me to tend to without a spiritual return on my religious investments. But that, I eventually discover, is also an impossible task. No matter how I attempt to exorcise even the mere demon idea of God, the absence of Him then begins to haunt me. From an untouchable God to no God at all, and still I am not satisfied.

❖ ❖ ❖

In the secret of His tabernacle, He will hide me. Oh taste and see that He is good. In the secret of his tabernacle He shall hide me. I will bless Him at all times. His praise shall be continually in my mouth. I have rested, I have waited patiently. My heart has been hot within me. I muse and the fire burns. His arrows stick fast in me, and His hand presses me sore. What am I that He is mindful of me? Oh—His kiss is like a prayer in my mouth.

❖ ❖ ❖

It is at the point of having nowhere else to turn that I turn finally inward, toward that looming and singular orchard and the landscape around it. I know it's there. I have known its presence even throughout my spasmodic attempts at this or that kind of worshipfulness. But I avoid it. *Why do I avoid it?* It's hard to get to, and the journey within is treacherous. *What if I get there and He doesn't show?* No one wants to be left alone and vulnerable, waiting. *What if I'm not good enough for God?* As if "good enough" has an accurate definition. *Oh Longings, what is it exactly that you are longing for?* The answer surprises even me in its candor, and it is this: I am looking for a sign, a bush or a body on fire. Something to fill the whole hole of it, my affordable black moods and the comfortable malaise of any unsignified life. Something satisfying, and deeply possible.

❖ ❖ ❖

He seduces me with a come-hither power that only very great men can manage. My bones are vexed. My bones tremble at the sight of Him over me. My bones belong to Him. He spreads out a cloud to cover me. Heaven bestows. A cherry hangs from its stem, from His fingers. Openings await.

❖ ❖ ❖

Psalm—even the word sounds sexual. *The palm of his hand and its balm, a small asp in secret, the lapse of alms giving, the same lap of God.* Do whatever word trickery that pleases you—the fluid, tongue-tactile, erotically pleasing blend of all those consonants hugging that one curious vowel (*a scarlet A, perhaps?*) witnesses a sensuality that translates into the poems themselves. Of all the things that the Psalms are, a striking unity presents: they are deeply, unashamedly personal. It is the voice of the singular I crying out to a God that sometimes consoles, sometimes chastens, and sometimes is nowhere to be found. The Psalms divulge an almost unfair intimacy. Even in His God-ness, His bigness, His universality, His hiddenness, His mystery—He *is*, and we are beholden to Him.

> Beneath the branch my flesh is sure—
> Not vindicated quite, not pure
> As infant snow—but mine—and firm
> Within His holy, hungry arms.
> Against the sinews of this tree
> He pours like water over me,
> And I am wet. The lily groans.
> Two bodies relent, bone for bone.
> The meadow overtakes the gates.
> My darkness is His secret place.

The first-person frankness of the Psalms discloses the openness of a surprisingly intimate relationship. *Me. I. Look at how I love You, Lord. Let me tell of all the things You have done for me. Where are You when I need you? Who and how will You destroy? For Thee I have sung to and sinned against.* The God the Psalms speak to is not a communal incarnation. No, it's the God of a solitary soul sitting in the dark of a room, the consort of a breathless woman heaving under a tree. In the traditional Christian liturgy, the call-and-response singing of the psalm is the one outstanding moment where the work of the people is turned into the work of the person. Even in the Order of Confession and Forgiveness (at least in the mainline Protestant church that I attend), it is the plural *we* who makes the confession, and at the altar, the *you* in "this is my body given for you" is presumed (rightly) to be a collective you, all of you. So the God of the Psalms is chiefly personal. It's that kind of God a person can write poems to and for, all kinds of poems—love poems, hate poems, poems of contrition, poems of belief and despair, real poems that hold tautly the legitimate tension in that sly, thin thread from which we all depend.

◆ ◆ ◆

He is wild, a little rough, a little vengeful, perhaps. A rabid dog, a snake, perhaps, a devil—I don't know what it is but it is something—leaps out at me from a mirage. He fights it down. He kills it with His own hands. He stands brave and all-powerful as I weep and rail in spasms it hurts to even name. From enemies seen and unseen, He will protect me. He lifts the hem of my dress with His hands. He leaves a stain upon me. I am marked. The shudder of it rattles at my inmost pleat.

◆ ◆ ◆

And who or what exactly is God in these poems? He's many things. He is the protector and champion of the faithful, true, but He is also quite able and quite ready to chasten those who follow Him, when they fall away, or when He perceives such a thing has happened. He is a gentle shepherd, but also an exacting master with cruel tendencies. He is a heavenly emperor, ruling all, and yet His power stops at the bounds of my free will. He is kind and jealous at once. He is the warrior, a bloody sword in his left hand, his right held out as an offering. He is the confidant to the troubled, and the trouble of those too confident. Most of anything, He is the ever-present object of the psalmist's affection, to be loved and to be feared.

It would be a grave mistake to deny God the cruelty and violence that the psalmist freely offers as one (not the only one, but certainly one) of His attributes. But how is this resolved? Is God evil? Certainly, He is presented here as fickle and stubborn. One answer is to simply point to the vengeance of God as an example of an antiquated understanding of justice. Another is to call to attention the change that seems to overtake God (in the Christian understanding at least) in the span between the Old and New Testaments. But that doesn't really resolve anything. The God of the New Testament still has a thirst for blood and sacrifice. Lest we forget that, remember that Jesus, in the midst of dying a criminal's tortured death, admits to the heavens—*Thy will be done*. One more approach to this apparent inconsistency is to shrug the shoulders and say, to no one in particular, Oh, that's just God, as if we were talking about an errant but mostly harmless lover on the scam. *He can't help it, He's built that way*—and in the saying of it, avoid coping with the reality that His wrath exists, and is troubling.

None of these answers satisfies me. What if—heresy of heresies— God is more like us than we care to admit, than we dare allow Him to be? What if His violent side, His petty side, and His meanness are instead manifestations of a tragic flaw, that one crack in His otherwise impeccable veneer, His singular imperfection? It is said that exceptions prove the rule. In that case, the flaw wouldn't deny God his God-ness but would instead affirm the natural truth of it. Like the arc of a brushstroke that identifies a Picasso canvas, perhaps His mutability and His moody anger is part of God's signature, his unique handwriting. As if God, in his absolute brightness, casts an equally impressive shadow. That is something to be dealt with. We just don't like to think He has it in Him. But it doesn't make me love Him any less. If anything, the darker sides of God attract me a little more to Him, the same way that the Czarina was drawn to Rasputin, or that any good woman's heart might flutter at the thought of being drawn into the fabulously rough arms of Steve McQueen. You have to put yourself a little more at the mercy of a God with a river of darkness roiling just underneath his muscles. However uncomfortable that might make us feel (and really, it should make us feel uncomfortable), to be able to look upon God with an honest eye allows Him true form, a real face and real hands.

◆ ◆ ◆

Rise up, oh Judge of the earth—judge me! He formed my eye and He sees it! He fought for the corners of my mouth and He hears the words they speak— marvelous, marvelous things He has done. I quake, I tremble. My hair is in His hands, my whole suffering self.

◆ ◆ ◆

I hold in my mind an image of David, King of Israel, bent over a small table in a dark room lit only by the short, burning wick of a lamp. His harem and his whole household are quiet. It is late into the night, closer to morning than evening. But David cannot sleep. There is a sword somewhere nearby. He is writing.

Of course, David didn't really write all the Psalms, but he is conflated with their authorship nonetheless, in the same way that the image of the Magdalene is by tradition tied forever to that of the adulterous woman and her wantonries. Still, I rather like to imagine David composing them, inventing them, channeling them, tucked over his scroll as the words come painfully out of his heart and onto the paper. I hold onto this somewhat factually erroneous image because in truth, no matter the genuine author, the Psalms are fully David's—the mad, garbled, glorious stutterings of a carnal man with personal carnage in the pockets and creases of his tunic. In that way, they belong to him. In that way, they belong to all who will admit to his or her own humanness. It is hard work to live under the conscious eye of God, that all-seeing, universal magnifying glass—us, the little ants getting crispy and charred in the funnel of its concentrated light. Somehow, David's holy desires are not undone by his unholy acts. In a way, one seems to legitimize the other. David is a man whose terrible deeds and their depth are outweighed only by his charisma and the favor that God bestows upon him. The Psalms belong to him. The Psalms belong to anyone who accepts the call to live a fully human life in the hopes that despite it (or, maddest of hopes, because of it) someone so great as the king of the universe would have her to be his own. On our best and worst days, we are—most of us—only a mirror's sorry reflection of either extreme. King David is dark and dangerous, and he's got the God to match.

◆ ◆ ◆

The days are like evening shadow, that He hides His face from me. I wither like the grass. I will surely die. A ripe plum left untouched will burst apart. Fruit is not quite fruit unless it is eaten.

✦ ✦ ✦

I falter at trying to imagine anything closer than the closeness of the physical sex act. Quite literally, it involves stepping into another person's skin. Areas of the body generally covered by clothing or convention are bared. Places in the inner heart that are kept from view are revealed in the same manner, gladly and with anxiousness both. There are fluids—blood, sweat, semen; unnameable juices and exotic aromas. And this is just the physical aspect that I consider here, not the emotional component, heavy and intrusive and, whether we want to acknowledge it or not, also present. In its metaphor, sexual intercourse is a union of opposites. The male and the female become a little of each other. Literally, therefore, sexual congress is a transformation. Symbolically, it's alchemical magic.

Using the imagery of sexual intention to interpret the experience of God is not an invention of my own. I point to the obvious—the longings of the mystic saints and their prayers, the Song of Solomon and the Church's standard (if prudish) interpretation of its erotic verses, the wooing of God's people to Him, the seduction and consummation of that relationship. Sexual imagery runs like a rampant metaphor in the pages of the Gospels, where through the example of Jesus we find and fall at the blood and bone of a physical, tangible being—all God and every inch a man. There's titillation in the idea that God can in all ways enter into our secret selves, that Christ can bleed entire agonies for the mere sake of some greater passion, that saints will come to know God through ecstasy alone and the gooseflesh on their breasts shall prove it, that the rest of us will fumble at buttons and clasps breathlessly between it all.

✦ ✦ ✦

The Psalms' words swim in the greatest depths, the uncharted longings of this desire, this brutal, beautiful, passionate sea that anyone who dares to follow God must, must row out into. The power of language cannot be accidental—words are spoken and worlds leap into existence, animals are named, and law is written on top of desert mountains. The poet's work—if she is honest with herself and if she is willing to do the work that the words themselves have deep within them—is the prophet's work. She announces that we can be a delight to God. She proclaims that God can be a delight to us. She makes it clear that all the mad, unfortunate stuff of life in between the two pleasures is necessary—pain and joy, to be sure, but most of all, every degree of longing that falls within the bounds of each extreme. The Psalms (and all true poems) remind us, if only in their feeling and not their form, that though we mortals can come very close to God, entering into the awe as well as the awful of God's presence, we can never become God. God is something other than us. He may be the beloved object of our empty or broken hearts growing full, but He is also a unique being, something, someone entirely separate from us. Two people make love, and they arrive as far into the other as is absolutely possible, but they don't become each other. But they do become, both of them, a new creation, something that neither of them could have managed on their own. The relationship changes them. God's relationship with us changes us. Perhaps it even changes God. In writing, too, a new thing is made. Something that can approach the feeling of it, whatever *it* is. Writing is a sexual act. In the poem, in the psalm, in lovemaking, what is real and what is imagined converge in the image of the hoped-for and longed-for Other. What rises out of this union is the true image of a very genuine and very present being in fantasy's real-life stead. We are impossibly unable to meet the demands of any ideal, written or otherwise. But how necessary for us to try!

A sexual union means more than two bodies bumping together, but there is meaning in just that. The God of the Psalms has a vicious beauty, a violent benevolence. In short, he is erotically invoked in words one would generally reserve for a lover. In this essay, I have chosen to retain the masculine, majuscule pronoun in honor of that. The ancient Hebrew understanding of God was clearly a male one, and truly, the image of God in the Psalms is virile. But even the early Israelites grasped that for creation to occur (human procreation, and likewise the birth of the universe) both sexes were indispensable. The Hebrew equivalent of the Mesopotamian goddess Ishtar (Ashtoreth, or Asharah) was widely, popularly regarded as the consort of Jehovah. Evidence of her cult can be seen even in the time of Solomon, where the inmost part of the temple, the Holy of Holies, carried the connotations of her womb, where mysteries rose up and a secret darkness called. The female aspect of the Judeo-Christian deity has since been absorbed into the image of His people. We—regardless of our gender—are God's women. I thrill a little to think of that. As Christ would later do so often and so well, the God of the Psalms meets us like maidens in the road. He places His hands upon us. He releases us from our baser human natures. But in return for that blessing, we are bound to Him, this wild erotic savior of a man, angry and brooding, and good beyond any way that we can imagine goodness to be. The paradox in that argument is this: *Could God be God without us?* And, *exactly how much pleasure does God derive from us, require of us?*

◆   ◆   ◆

In my own writing, I think, I've been pressed into the service of the Word quite accidentally. My faith life, as I have pointed out, has inconsistency as its hallmark, but when I am on fire for God, I burn white-hot. I have discovered that my creativity and my spirituality are knotted tightly together. The holiest I ever feel (and the sexiest too) is when I am writing, or have just written. The more I write, the more I rely on it for my wholeness. And, in the end, it doesn't seem to be the final product that brings the pleasure, but the work itself. Working, writing, is an intimate act between God and me. There is struggle, there is pleasure, and there is release. It's communion without the altar rail. Poems stain the sheets upon our marriage bed. This is how God and I get to know each other. And I do mean *know*. In the biblical sense.

◆   ◆   ◆

When passion is tortured no more, when my skin has burned away from my bones, when my true self is known and named, when the day turns dusk and the sky hushes quietly the wind, when His arms wrap around me in such a way as to hold me as I have never been held, never will be held by any other, when the ease of my groin rests peacefully, when the cherries have been eaten and praised—I am satisfied. I have seen—I have loved—the Lord and lived to tell it.

✦ ✦ ✦

It doesn't have to be a cherry tree. It doesn't have to be a tree at all. But it can be, and God can be the one who meets you underneath. At least that's my fantasy. But God really isn't a fantasy, and anyway, fantasies of God are whole, tortured steps removed from His very hands grasping at my upper arms. It's not a happy little world, this earth which hangs oddly like a round swollen fruit, spinning from the branch of that tree we cannot name. And if it were a trite, content place, it would come with its own dissatisfaction. True pleasure can only survive in the presence or at least the real possibility of true pain. At the center of the cherry is the pit. In the end, a heart full of God finds itself possessed by the object of its very own obsession. That's a dark, a dangerous love. That's a love that bites back.

And what's wrong, exactly, with praying to a God who will have me, all of me, deliberately, deeply?

> *In Thy right hand there are pleasures.*
> *In Thy left hand there are pleasures.*
> *Let Zion be the cleave of my soul's sighing thighs.*

PSALM 22 AND THE GOSPELS
A Midrashic Moment and a Hope for Connection

Enid Dame

Abraham Joshua Heschel has said that poetry, in contrast to philosophy, is "a self-sufficing pouring forth of insight" rather than "an attempt to offer an answer to a problem."[1] Of course, this "insight," when shared with an audience of readers or listeners—in whom it may trigger insights of their own—can in itself begin the process that leads to solutions. Or it can simply offer the comforting knowledge that one is not alone in a hostile universe, that others have encountered similar "problems" before and have responded, however well or badly.

The power of the Psalms lies in their ability to reach out to us down through the centuries, to assure us that another person has experienced profound sorrow, betrayal, or illness and has captured this experience in startlingly precise language and imagery. The largest number of psalms belong to this category—laments, or prayers for help. Perhaps the strongest and most intriguing of these is Psalm 22, both for its stunning presentation of a state of personal despair and alienation, which is later overcome and replaced by a sense of connection with God, family, and community, and for its resilience, its ability to time-travel out of its own period and reappear, in various forms, in very different works of literature and art.

In the late nineteenth century, for example, it becomes a beloved Jewish song, "Eyli Eyli," which rivals the liturgical Kol Nidre in popularity, offering cultural solace to generations of Jewish immigrants to America.[2] Its first line leaps out of Allen Ginsberg's "Howl," and its imagery of rejection and persecution are echoed in the "confessional" poetry of Anne Sexton (see, for example, "The Death Baby"). But certainly the most dramatic and culturally significant reconfiguration

49

of this poem is its role in the New Testament, where all four Gospel writers weave its language and imagery directly into their scenes of the crucifixion.

As John Shelby Spong tells us, "These accounts are illustrative . . . of the process by which the life of Jesus was incorporated into and interpreted by the traditions of the Jewish past."[3] Indeed, the Gospel writers, three of whom were Jews (and the fourth, Luke, was well-versed in Jewish tradition) composed their accounts "with their Hebrew Bibles open," expanding on particular passages, "for that was the only way their vocabulary allowed them to speak of the holy God."[4] In other words, they were writing midrash.

Midrash is a unique Jewish literary genre in which biblical texts are imaginatively interpreted, expanded upon, and even reapplied to other biblical passages. Gary Porton, in "One Definition of Midrash," identifies several "propositions" on which rabbinic midrash is based, three of which are relevant to this discussion. First, since the Scriptures were believed to be "an accurate and complete public record" of God's revelations to his people, "nothing in the Bible was unimportant or superfluous."[5] Moreover, since all biblical passages were believed to be interrelated, "a section of the Prophets may be used to explain a verse from the Torah, or a portion of the Torah may explain a passage from the writings."[6] Finally, "any given biblical verse was open to more than one possible interpretation."[7] One rabbi's—or modern reader's—midrash does not replace or cancel out another's.

As a Jewish poet whose work draws deeply on biblical images and narratives, I find midrash an essential way to approach the texts of the Bible. It is an approach I use in my Bible as Literature courses at New Jersey Institute of Technology (NJIT) and Rutgers University. The glory of midrash, and of a "midrashic approach" to the Bible, is that one story opens out into many stories; the possibilities of fresh interpretations are limitless—and all are valuable. This approach allows a class of students from various religious backgrounds to read or reread the Bible without falling down familiar rabbit holes: arguments about which reading is "better," mini–holy wars, insistence that there is but one "correct" way to respond to a given passage.

As Spong shows us, this process actually extends not only as a linkage between passages in the Jewish Bible but as a series of linkages between the Jewish Bible and the New Testament. Certainly Psalm 22's reappearance in the Gospels constitutes a "midrashic moment," a conscious incorporation of an early text into a later one. While traditional readings suggest a political or triumphalist agenda (which are undeniably in operation), I wish to offer another, rather different way of reading this particular midrash.

All four Gospel writers turned to Psalm 22 for inspiration, imagery, and even dialogue when attempting to imagine the scene of the crucifixion. We may ask: Why did they choose this psalm in particular? What is the nature of its power?

Psalm 22 starts as a lament and finally becomes a song of praise. Considered to be written by David, its instructions "To the leader: according to the Deer of the Dawn" may suggest that it was sung to a particular melody. However, the Septuagint translates this phrase as "Concerning the help at dawn."[8] This interpretation is emotionally appealing; the poem does indeed read as a cry for help during the early morning of a long soul-wrenching night.

The speaker in the first line calls out poignantly to the God he feels has deserted him: "My God, my God, why have you forsaken me?" This is the line that reverberates, sweeping the reader along, whatever her culture or century, encapsulating our loneliness and yearning for connection, our need to address a God we suspect may not be listening. In verses 3–5, the speaker reminds himself that God *was* there for his ancestors. Unlike them, he feels cast out, "a worm," "not human" (22:6). Then he introduces a powerful theme: he is taunted by others, who mock his faith, saying sarcastically, "Commit your cause to the Lord; let him deliver" (22:7–8). Their words appear to have some effect, as he next reasserts his belief in God as a protector: "Yet it was you who took me from the womb; / you kept me safe on my mother's breast" (22:9).

Reminding us that birth in itself is a perilous undertaking, these lines also, amazingly, depict God as a midwife, a sheltering motherly force:

> On you I was cast from my birth,
> and since my mother bore me
> you have been my God. (22:20)

Having established this relationship with God to be long-standing, he asks God to be present for him now "when there is no one to help" (22:11).

This picture of complete powerlessness is expanded on in the next verses in a series of stunning images. "Strong bulls of Bashan," who are themselves compared to a "ravening and roaring lion" (22:12–13) confront him. The speaker goes numb: "I am poured out like water" (22:14). His body becomes unfamiliar: "All my bones are out of joint" (22:14). He is close to death, but, even worse, he is defeated and humiliated: metaphoric dogs surround him; hostile individuals, "evildoers," not only "gloat" over his predicament but cruelly and visibly make plans to appropriate his clothing after his death by casting lots (22:16–18).

A shift occurs in verse 19: the speaker calls on God once again; he pleads to be rescued, and deliverance comes, suddenly, like a saving downpour of rain in the middle of verse 21 (indicated by white space in the modern text):

> Save me from the mouth of the lion!
>
> From the horns of the wild oxen you have rescued me.

The poem now becomes a hymn of thanksgiving, the psalmist joyfully stating his intention to praise God to other members of his community (which he has now symbolically found, or rejoined): "I will tell of your name to my brothers and sisters; in the midst of the congregation, I will praise you" (22:22). In the actual praise song, the psalmist enjoins "All you offspring of Jacob" to "glorify" and "stand in awe" of the God who "did not hide his face" from the afflicted and despairing speaker (22:23–24). His triumph and joy are not individual, private emotions; they must be shared with and repeated by a "congregation" of fellow believers. Further, "all the ends of the earth" are invoked, and as the psalmist pictures the entire world worshipping the God who—in the poem's first political reference—is seen as ruling "over the nations" (22:27–28).

In the concluding verses, all the generations of the world, both the dead ("all who sleep in the earth") and the yet unborn ("future generations"), are united in their commitment to the God who brought the psalmist out of the depths of his alienation and despair into a world of connection: with family, community, congregation, nation, past and future. God, of course, is the primary connection, the connection that becomes the bridge out of the realm of self-loathing and spiritual death, the link that makes the others possible.

This is no facile panacea, but a profoundly comforting vision that echoes in our own time, as seen by its reappearance in contemporary poetry. It is understandable that poets like Ginsberg and Sexton, who wrote powerfully of traumatic psychological disconnections in the post–World War II era, would respond to this poem. And it is even less surprising that this psalm would reverberate in an earlier period of upheaval, instability, and loosening of familiar communal bonds: the period in which the Gospels were written.

Before looking at the ways in which strands of Psalm 22 reappear in the Gospels, however, it is necessary to talk about myself, to examine my own relationship to these texts, to this particular "midrashic moment." For, while Psalm 22 is definitely and radiantly a part of my own culture, the Gospels are not. Or are they?

Spong talks of reading the Gospels "with Jewish eyes." To me, as a Jewish reader, this approach makes supreme sense. But there's another issue: how do I, as a Jew, read the Gospels? It is possible to read them as literature rather than doctrine? Do I, as a reader, a student and teacher of literature, a Jewish poet, a Jew, have a stake in this story? Should I be reading it at all?

Until I was nine, my family lived in a series of working-class towns in western Pennsylvania and Ohio, the "tri-state area." Most of the residents were, of course, Christians. My parents, while not traditionally "observant," were deeply connected to their Jewish culture. In Beaver

Falls, Pennsylvania, where we lived at two different times, my father taught Sunday School (yes, Sunday, not Saturday—he, like most fathers, had to work on Saturday) in the Reform Temple, which met in a gray-painted frame house. The characters in the Bible were part of our family; Adam, Eve, King David, and Queen Esther joined us in the kitchen and were part of our dinnertime conversations. The first midrash I ever heard was my mother's spirited defense of Eve.

Though we lived in its midst and to some extent absorbed its culture, Christianity rarely entered our home. It was almost never discussed. At some point, I grasped that our religion was different from that of the other people in our world. Assuming that God was more or less the same for everyone, I asked my mother whom God liked better—"us" or "them." Her response was uncharacteristically straightforward: "Well, just between you and me, he really likes us better. But don't say that to your Christian friends. You don't want to make them angry."

I did have Christian friends. The stereotypical Jewish child's trauma of being victimized by anti-Semitic taunts and accusations never happened to me. On the contrary, I was able to find a place in the weave of neighborhood children in our various towns: Beaver Falls, Steubenville, New Brighten. In Beaver Falls, especially, I encountered a warm and gregarious neighborhood and grade school community, where I established bonds with two "best friends," Connie and Linda, as well as with other girls and even with a boy, Terry. All of these children were, of course, Christians. Until third grade, I was the only Jew in the school.

(I did have one Jewish girlfriend, the only other girl in my Sunday School class. My father would drive me across town—or was it to another town?—to visit her. We liked each other, but there was something a little formal in these visits—like her mother's carefully arranged sofa cushions, which could not actually be sat on. These engagements were very different from the spontaneous day-to-day life with the Catholic and Protestant children in my own neighborhood.)

These children included me in their community—yet there were limits. Certain words, I sensed, had walls around them. They were like packages; they had to be handled gingerly or they might explode. There were references, usually in tones of awed familiarity, to God, but also to various other personages. Who were they? I felt I could not ask; that would be like shaking the package. Their God seemed at times identical to ours: a vast, impersonal force whom you could, nevertheless, call on for support, as David did in the Psalms (as in, "Oh, God, let me pass this test," or "Please, God, let my mother come home from the hospital"). But there also was a person, a man-figure, who, like ordinary people, appeared to have a first and a last name—but who also seemed to be identified with God. How could this be? Our God was invisible; only Moses could see him, and *he* only was allowed to see a small part. Even more confusingly, my friends' god-man figure was sometimes described as a Jew, as King of the Jews, or—in a Christmas carol we all had to sing—"King of Israel"—words that belonged to my family. What on earth did this person have to do with our words, with us?

I remember one excruciating episode in the second grade. For some reason (in these pre–Madalyn Murray days) the teacher elected to tell us the story of Easter. Actually, she assumed we all knew it and thus did not provide any background or context. Her account of the Passion was quite graphic. (I still remember gruesome details of nails being driven through human flesh.) The class grew hushed; clearly my classmates were experiencing a deep collective emotion which I could not share. I felt locked outside an invisible edifice her words were erecting. In my memory, the room seemed to darken. The presence of other Jewish people in the story must have been confusing to me, though I do not remember a specific anti-Semitic interpretation, nor did anyone appear to connect the story with me. Rather, I felt erased from the class, profoundly excluded, and silenced. What exactly was happening? What was this story about? Why was the principal character—again, was he a man or a god?—being tortured, then killed? Was he a bad person, a criminal? I wanted to ask these questions, but knew that if I did, the room—my circle of friends and classmates—would turn unfriendly, turn against me. I sat in silence letting the waves of this story roll over me. I knew I could never ask anyone about what I was hearing: not the teacher, not my friends, not my parents.

Why not my parents? We could and did discuss many topics—my parents were ardent talkers and analyzers. Except for the early conversation with my mother about "us," "them," and God, we rarely discussed Christianity or our position as Jews in a decidedly non-Jewish culture. These topics, I sensed, were off-limits here as well.

I gained a revealing glimpse into the depth of my parents' anxiety about these subjects when I was twelve and going through an intense adolescent religious period. By this time, we had moved into Pittsburgh and joined another, more formally organized Reform Temple. To help deal with the pressures and demands of junior high (and with my body's astonishing changes), I had taken to saying spontaneous prayers at various times of day, and at night, in bed, before going to sleep. The God I addressed was indisputably the Jewish God, or a version of this deity—the God of David and Psalm 22. However, to make the night-time prayers more special, I usually folded my hands as the children did back in the mill town. It seemed to me that folded hands would be a pleasing social gesture, one God would appreciate—as a hostess might appreciate a personal thank-you note on nice stationery.

My parents walked in on one of these conversations and were appalled. They responded as if betrayed. As they saw it, I was "praying like a Christian"; therefore, another person, an older person, a "Christian," must be trying to convert me. It was an awkward moment. I knew I had hurt my parents and felt ashamed and guilty. It was difficult to find words to assure them that what they assumed was not the case. What was more upsetting, however, was not what I "exposed" to them—my desperate need of help from an outside source, a Higher Power—but what they revealed to me: the enormity of their fears and insecurity as Jews in diaspora. The worst fate they could imagine for their daughter was, apparently, "conversion": that is, being lost to them, completely losing contact with one's culture and family.

So those were the possible modes in which it seemed possible for Jews and Christians to interact with each other: opposition ("They'll be angry"), silence and erasure (why *did* that teacher introduce that story as she did knowing there was a Jewish child in the room?), or attempts at conversion. These stances certainly affect the way we read—or misread, or fail to read—the different parts of the Bible. In my Bible as Literature classes, students from Christian backgrounds often project their own "readings" backward onto the Old Testament in ways that undermine or erase the fact that, in Spong's words, "the Gospels are Jewish books,"[9] whose characters, including the protagonist, are Jewish products of a Jewish culture. Many Jews, including my literate parents, do not read the New Testament at all, fearing intense antagonism, demonization, or an attempt to seduce them away from their deepest beliefs. Father Daniel Harrington speaks to this dual resistance in a perceptive essay, "Retrieving the Judaism of Jesus: Recent Developments," when he says, "Some Christians still instinctively resist calling Jesus a Jew, and some Jews regard Jesus as an apostate who does not deserve to be called a Jew."[10]

Given these traditional antagonisms, is there any hope that we can read each other's texts and see them as related in ways that increase our mutual knowledge rather than embracing or rejecting the other, sibling religion? Of course there is; Harrington's essay appears in a book, *The Historical Jesus through Jewish and Christian Eyes*, dedicated to just this trend in biblical studies. However, it is another Beaver Falls story that I would like to call upon to illustrate the possibility of connections rather than divisions between readers of our related texts.

As I mentioned before, the Beaver Falls Reform Temple met in a gray frame house; it stood across the street from a rather imposing gray stone church. One Sunday I discovered a classmate (not one of my close friends) coming out of this building. We greeted each other warily—at first.

"What are you doing here?" she asked.

"I go to Sunday School here." I indicated the house.

"Oh, so do I!" She indicated her building. "What are you doing now, in your class?"

"Oh, we're doing Noah."

"Noah? Gee! So are we."

We laughed together in a kind of relieved amazement. How surprising—how comforting—to know we were reading and discussing the same text in our different gray buildings of worship on different corners of the street.

This was, for me, a moment of profound connection. At that time, it seemed enough of a revelation that we could be reading the same stories in our different classrooms. It didn't occur to me then, of course, that our stories, our Noahs, could be different—or that we could learn from each other's versions.

However, this incident started the process in my life which led to my eventually teaching Bible as Literature classes to students from various religious backgrounds, and to the discovery, along with a particularly perceptive Summer Session class at NJIT, of a perfect example of a "midrashic moment" in Psalm 22's stunning reappearance in the New Testament.

Psalm 22 is employed in all four Gospels, where it functions as "one of the primary sources for the crucifixion narrative."[11] It is instructive to examine the specific aspects of the psalm that the four Gospel writers selected for use in their own texts.

Perhaps the most conspicuous borrowing, appearing in all four Gospels in similar form, is the detail of the soldiers who cast lots for the crucified Jesus' clothing. In the psalm, it is the speaker's tormentors who do this, while he is near death, but still alive: "They divide my clothes among themselves, / and for my clothing they cast lots" (Psalm 22:18). In this psalm, this is the culminating image in a series that metaphorically represents the speaker's growing sense of anguish and desolation. First, the speaker imagines himself weakening ("poured out like water"), afflicted by illness ("all my bones are out of joint"), surrounded by enemies ("a company of evildoers encircles me"). It is while he is in this near-death state (a decline closely linked to the malice of his enemies) that these persecutors gleefully, in his presence, make plans to appropriate his clothes after his death. The point here is that these people are callously and consciously treating him as if he is *already* dead, thus nullifying his humanity, reinforcing his state of alienation.

This nightmarish metaphor of ultimate erasure, of death-in-life, is transformed in the Gospels to a literal plot-detail: Roman soldiers are depicted, in all four texts, as actually casting lots for Jesus' clothing after

his execution. Mark presents the episode—as it has now become—
with his usual matter-of-factness: "And they crucified him, and divided
his clothes among them, casting lots to decide what each should take"
(Mark 15:24). Matthew and Luke essentially repeat Mark, not placing
much emphasis on this story; for them it is one detail among many.
John gives a much fuller account (19:23–25), explaining that there were
four soldiers and that each took one part of Jesus' clothes. But since they
could not easily divide his seamless tunic, they decided to cast lots for
it. Then John explicitly calls our attention to what he is doing here; the
soldiers' actions are done "to fulfill what the scripture says" (19:24). John
is alluding of course to Psalm 22, which he then quotes, adding, "And
that is what the soldiers did" (19:25).

A question arises: why does this particular image (as opposed to, say,
the bulls of Bashan or the vicious dogs) achieve such prominence in the
Gospels? In using this psalm, John is obviously drawing a link between
Jesus and his illustrious ancestor David the psalmist, thus reinforcing
his claim that Jesus is the Messiah (who, in Jewish tradition, would be
descended from the great King of Israel). While the other three Gospel
writers would share his agenda (and assume that a Jewish readership
would catch the allusion to the psalm), they are more indirect, employ-
ing the image as a "vivid" or "telling" detail, an aspect of telling a good
story. One might assume that this image would logically appeal to all
four writers because, unlike the images of violent animals, it appears
realistic (could it be based on an actual wartime practice?), an event that
could plausibly take place in the scene they were imagining.

In other words, the "insight" of the poet into a psychologically bleak
state of mind has become transformed by the Gospel storytellers into
an element of prose narrative: a "telling" detail for Mark, Matthew, and
Luke, a mechanism of foreshadowing for John. Interestingly, Jesus *him-
self* cannot see or respond to this indignity; he does not need to. It is
clearly there to enhance or guide the *reader's* reaction to the story.

The other aspect of Psalm 22 that appears in all four Gospels, though
here each writer makes significant changes, is the presence of the mock-
ers. Much of the power of Psalm 22 (as in similar laments) lies in the

depiction of these tormentors, who are compared, as we have seen, to wild and dangerous beasts: bulls, lions, dogs, oxen. In verse 8, the psalmist actually quotes one of his tormentor's sarcastic taunts: "Commit your cause to the Lord; let him deliver—let him rescue the one in whom he delights!"

In the psalm, it is the speaker's sense of powerlessness and vulnerability which come across. The identity of the mockers is not emphasized, nor are they associated with any particular social, religious, or political group. While they do taunt the speaker for his belief in a protective God, their own religious beliefs—or lack of them—are not explicit. Indeed, they speak of "the Lord" rather than "your Lord"; they could nominally share the speaker's religion; they could represent aspects of his own doubt and self-loathing. One suspects it is this very lack of specificity that gives this psalm its power, its ability to travel through time, to resonate in other centuries and cultures: it really doesn't matter *who* these scoffers are; we have all encountered them in one voice or another, including our own.

In the Gospels, once again, we see a transformation of poetry into prose narrative. The mockers are no longer generalized figures, but very specific players in the story. In Mark, they are divided into three groups: the Roman soldiers who strike Jesus, spit on him, and salute him in mock homage (15:18–20), an anonymous crowd of derisive passersby (15:30), and the chief priests and scribes, who jeer, "He saved others, he cannot save himself" (15:31). Matthew, who obviously used Mark as a source, continues this pattern, adding a few touches of his own. Not only do soldiers, passersby, priests, and scribes mock Jesus, but the bandits about to be crucified with him join in as well (27:44). Furthermore, the number of spoken taunts has increased. Luke is more aware of nuances. He describes a group of "chief priests, the officers of the temple police and the elders" who seize, mock, and physically assault Jesus (22:54, 63–65). But in depicting the actual crucifixion scene, Luke carefully distinguishes between the crowd of people—presumably Jews—who are highly sympathetic to Jesus (23:27; the women actually beat their breasts and wail) and their hostile leaders.

John briefly depicts the Roman soldiers mocking and assaulting "the King of the Jews" (19:3), but his emphasis is reserved for other aspects of the story: the zeal of the Temple priests to see Jesus executed and Pilate's equivocal role in the proceedings.

How does a Jewish reader enter these texts? How, for example, might my mother have read them? I picture her entering the story warily, suspiciously, like a cat in a new house, sniffing at the words, which seem both familiar and strange. Once she got her bearings, however, she might point out that the generalized enemies and scorners of the poem, those familiar demons of the psyche, have now been identified as *political* opponents: Romans, religious authorities, temple police. She would be appalled, but not really surprised, at how often and intensely (especially in John) these unpleasant characters, the villains of the story, are identified as Jews. Here she might say, "This is enemy territory!" Or simply turn and flee.

Or, since she was interested in the workings of history, she might, later, consult books that construct the events of this period to provide context for the Gospel stories. Spong, for example, reminds us that the later three Gospels were written after the Roman war against the Jews and the fall of the Temple in Jerusalem, pointing out that the ultimate break between Jews and Jewish Christians (or "followers of the way" within Judaism; they did not call themselves "Christians" yet) was a direct result of those cataclysmic events. After the fall of their Temple—the focal point for Jewish religious observance—Judaism became focused on survival. This meant an increased role for the rabbinate (the Pharisees of the Christian story), who evolved a new version of the religion centering not on temple observances, which must be carried out by priests, but on dynamic small groups of worshippers led by rabbis (teachers), and based on a strict interpretation of the Torah—now the centerpiece of the religion. While before the destruction of the Temple, Judaism could and did tolerate Jesus' followers as radical reformers within their community, it now saw them as a threat to survival. For their part, the "followers of the way" saw the fall of the Temple as "God's punishment of the Jerusalem Jews for their rejection of Jesus."[12] Thus, wider historical events sealed the fates of both "peoples" as enemies. It is this bitterness that we see in some of the language of the Gospels, in the tension that percolates between our two related religions even today.

Harrington addresses this issue in his essay, stating that "Christians are obliged to face up to the tendencies in the Gospels to blame Jews and exculpate Romans for Jesus' death," and recommends that both Jews and Christians today approach these writings with "a sense of history."[13] He locates many of these "tendencies" in the book of Matthew, which, in his opinion, is at once the most Jewish and most anti-Jewish Gospel.[14] While I personally, as a Jewish reader, feel much more alienated by John's presentation of the crucifixion (and respond positively to much of Matthew's portrayal of Jesus as a person very much connected to his Jewish background—a sort of radical Reform rabbi of his time), I find Harrington's analysis quite useful here, especially as it touches directly on Psalm 22.

It is Matthew, of course, who constructs a genealogy in which Jesus is directly linked to the family whose stories we follow through the Hebrew Scriptures; Abraham, Isaac, Jacob, Judah and Tamar, Ruth and Boaz, King David are all his ancestors. But he also, in his numerous references to the Jewish Bible, is obviously claiming—or rewriting— the earlier texts to support what was in the process of becoming an entirely separate religion. According to Harrington, in a world where survival of Judaism was uncertain, Matthew was trying to show that the heritage of the Jews would be best preserved by accepting Jesus as "the authoritative interpreter of the Torah." To support his position, Matthew constantly reminds his Jewish audience that Jesus died "according to the scriptures"—especially Psalm 22, "the psalm of the righteous sufferer."[15] Here, midrash is employed to serve what may be called a religious-political agenda: providing justification to a Jewish readership to accept this new religion rather than follow the Pharisees (who are denigrated in this Gospel) and their attempt to preserve the old one. Thus Matthew's debates with his opponents "take on the appearance of an intense religious family feud" like those between Catholics and Protestants in a later period.[16] Harrington concludes, with a piece of

good advice to modern readers: "There is no need to transfer a first cen-
tury family feud with Judaism to the twentieth century."[17]

However, it is not easy for the survivors of this "feud" to transcend
it, even in the twenty-first century. As Leonard Greenspoon, coedi-
tor of *The Historical Jesus through Jewish and Christian Eyes*, says, "For
many Jews, any reference to the New Testament and to Jesus, even a
Jewish Jesus, is a turn-off. Too many times we have been bombarded
by a 'Christian' message that denigrates our faith by contrasting the
eternal nature of the new covenant with the supposedly outmoded
status of the old."[18] His analysis certainly explains my parents' reaction
to what they—mistakenly—saw as an attempt to "convert" me. It also
explains the invisible barriers I have felt most of my life between Jews
and Christians (even when we are neighbors, classmates, "best friends"),
between the Old and the New Testaments. It explains the reluctance or
even apprehension I originally felt when approaching the Gospels, even
as "literary" texts. Was I betraying my culture, taking the wrong side in
a "family feud"? Yet I also felt an intense curiosity, a sense that they were
indeed part of my "family story"—part of my cultural heritage as a Jew,
a text I must enter and try to understand.

The third borrowing from Psalm 22 in the Gospels may suggest a way
out of this impasse. The strongest and most resonant reappearance, of
course, is that of its stunning first line: "My God, my God, why have you
forsaken me?" This plea, arguably the most powerful part of the poem,
grants us immediate entrance into the psalmist's mind and emotional
state. Two of the Gospel writers, Mark and Matthew, seize on this cry
of despair and employ it in a very significant way in their accounts of
the crucifixion story.

Since the story itself, naturally enough, is presented *as* a story, a nar-
rative, for the most part, we see what is happening from without. Each
Gospel writer emphasizes different aspects, but all give panoramic views
of the events as they affect others: the Roman soldiers, the crowd (usu-
ally hostile, though sympathetic in Luke), the high priests, the temple
police, Pilate, Judas, the followers and family members, the thieves, the
centurion. This is a good strategy, recognized by all creative writing teach-

ers, in composing an imagined scene: *showing* rather than simply *telling* us what is happening by recording reactions of various participants or onlookers. However, the one "point of view" we do not enter into for much of the story is that of its protagonist. Jesus himself seems strangely remote from the events swirling around him. The other borrowings from Psalm 22 reinforce this distance—for Jesus, unlike the psalmist, is not expressing his feelings. We do not know how he felt about the mocking soldiers, crowd or priests, for example. (Does he share our indignation? Or is he unconcerned with such trivial matters as human rudeness and cruelty?) The scene for the most part is presented in terms of actions observed, not "interiority," to use Robert Alter's word. As we have seen before, a poem has been reconfigured to serve the needs of prose.

But this is not true of the first line of the psalm. By directly putting the psalmist's words into Jesus' mouth, Mark brilliantly gives us a glimpse of insight into his protagonist's personal feelings. Matthew, the most connected to his Jewish roots, repeats it in a context that intensifies Jesus' own connection with these roots. (Luke and John, incidentally, assign different "last words" to Jesus, for, as Spong points out, they are emphasizing different points.)[19]

I suggest that, in this act of borrowing, both Mark and Matthew are responding primarily as writers, makers of literature, allowing us to imagine a Jesus who, like the psalmist and like those of us who have suffered through our own successive time periods with their outbreaks of war, massacres, holocausts, terrorist attacks on the city we thought invulnerable, continues to talk to the God he feels (and we feel) may not be listening. Significantly, it is a *poem* that is recalled here as the best possible way to express deep, almost inexpressible feelings. In this moment, the protagonist of the Gospels seems to be at his most poignantly and profoundly human.

Furthermore, he can be seen here as at his most Jewish—an anguished Jewish man spontaneously turning to the poetry of his ancestors, if not his illustrious Ancestor, to convey his feelings both of utter desolation and loneliness, and an implicit belief that God *will* eventually respond. It is in this moment—this superb example of a "midrashic moment"—that

Jesus, the Jesus portrayed by Mark and Matthew, seems most linked to his sources, his own culture and tradition.

Also, because so many people—Jews, Christians, and others— have found solace and support in this psalm, this can also be seen as a moment of profound universal connection. The psalm records a journey from the depths of isolation back into community, into a series of linkages between ancestors and succeeding generations. I suggest that this midrashic reading of Mark's and Matthew's application of the psalmist's words can give us a moment of "insight"—to use Heschel's term—which may serve to cement the ties between, rather than to separate, the members of the two "familial" religions who continue to read and respond to these texts. Further, this creative melding of poetry into prose, old story into a new one might give us hope that our own "unborn generations"— the family members we haven't met yet—will find new ways to read and learn from each other's words.

NOTES

1. Abraham Joshua Heschel, *God in Search of Man: A Philosophy of Judaism* (New York: Noonday Press, 1955), 4.

2. Irving Saposnik, "Jolson, Judy, and Jewish Memory," *Judaism* 50.4 (Fall 2001): 410–25; quote is from 417.

3. John Shelby Spong, *Liberating the Gospels: Reading the Bible with Jewish Eyes* (New York: HarperCollins, 1997), 48.

4. Ibid., 249.

5 Gary Porton, "One Definition of Midrash," in *Midrash as Literature*, ed. Jacob Neusner (Lanham, MD: University Press of America), 225–29; quote is from 227.

6 Ibid., 227–28.

7 Ibid., 228.

8 Wayne Meeks, ed., *The HarperCollins Study Bible (New Revised Standard Edition)* (London: HarperCollins, 1993), 818n.

9 Spong, *Liberating the Gospels*, 23.

10. Daniel Harrington, S.J., "Retrieving the Judaism of Jesus: Recent Developments," in *The Historical Jesus through Jewish and Christian Eyes*, ed. Bryan F. Le Beau, Leonard Greenspoon, and Dennis Hamm, S.J. (Harrisburg, PA: Trinity Press, 2000), 67.

11. Spong, *Liberating the Gospels*, 11.

12. Ibid., 46.

13. Harrington, "Retrieving the Judaism of Jesus," 79.

14. Ibid., 80.

15. Ibid., 81.

16. Ibid.

17. Ibid., 82.

18. Leonard Greenspoon, Epilogue to *The Historical Jesus through Jewish Eyes*, ed. Bryan F. Le Beau, Leonard Greenspoon, and Dennis Hamm, S.J. (Harrisburg, PA: Trinity Press, 2000), 169.

19. Spong, *Liberating the Gospels*, 249.

OF TIME AND VISION

Pattiann Rogers

In looking back over my published work of twenty-five years, I find that in eight poems I have used words directly from the Bible as either epigraphs or titles. Two of these references are from the Psalms—Psalm 1:2–3 and Psalm 23:4, both of which I will quote later. All six of the references are from the King James translation, and they ring to me with the sound and subtlety of poetry. In addition to the verses from the Psalms, the other six references are: "Consider the lilies of the field; they toil not, neither do they spin" (Matthew 6:28); "Though your sins be as scarlet they shall become as white snow" (Isaiah 1:18); "If a son shall ask bread of any of you that is a father, will he give him a stone? or if he ask a fish, will he for a fish give him a serpent?" (Luke 11:11); "In my Father's house are many mansions" (John 14:2); "the tongues of angels" (I Corinthians 13:1); "faith, hope, and charity" (I Corinthians 13:13).

I grew up with the sound of the King James Bible. I was urged to memorize many specific verses when I was young. Other verses I simply heard so often that I learned them by heart. The music of these verses is immersed in my language. The sound of these words and the stance they offer toward human experience have always seemed to me clearly capable of touching the contemporary heart. Yet writing in the latter half of the twentieth century, I have lived in a world invested with the images, the energy, the beauty, the tools, and the vocabulary of science. I am fascinated by the many descriptions of the physical world and its life processes and the total vision of the universe presented to us by the sciences—elementary particles, atoms and molecules, net-winged beetles and tall grass prairies, kelpfish and blue whales, sun bears and warthogs, clusters of galaxies and cosmic nebulae. At the same time, I am affected by language patterns in the Bible as part of my literary and religious heritage. I have wished to reconcile these powerful forces—the vision of life and the physical world being revealed by the sciences and the aspirations and spiritual yearnings expressed in the poetry of the Bible and in other arts. I have wanted the contemporary experience of the universe and our expressions of spiritual awareness to be in union. I feel they are in union, but that union has not always been fully realized or enunciated. Occasionally I have tried to describe the melding of these differing strengths in the music of words. I have attempted to accomplish this task without slighting the importance or the veracity of either realm of human experience.

Among the poems I've written, only one has begun from a dream. It was a very brief dream directly related to two verses from the first psalm, the words of which I could hear in my dream, although I did not speak them.

> 2   But his delight is in the law of the lord; and in his law doth he meditate day and night.
> 3   And he shall be like a tree planted by the rivers of water that bringeth forth his fruit in his season; his leaf also shall not wither; and whatsoever he doeth shall prosper.

In my dream, my father, who at the time of this dream had already passed away, was standing by a fence. I was very excited. I said to him, "I know now what these words mean!" When I woke, I had no idea why I had said this. I had never in the past puzzled particularly about the meaning of these two verses. They had always seemed fairly straightforward, containing a nice metaphor, the righteous person as a flourishing tree. I might have been mildly troubled by the idea that anyone should, or could, meditate on the Scriptures day and night to the exclusion of other sources of experience and knowledge. And I suppose it had also seemed unrealistic to me that anyone should actually "delight" in spending day and night in such meditation. But I accepted the fact that probably my temperament didn't allow me to understand fully the nature of that delight.

The aura of this dream lingered, as the aura of dreams sometimes will. I don't believe that dreams are prophetic or that they contain profound messages. But I was curious about this dream and motivated to investigate its assertion, to begin a poem with the hope of discovering, or creating, the "meaning" of these verses, the meaning I had spoken of in my dream.

The verses had given me some wonderful images to begin with—the river, the tree—and I had the delightful word "delight." And I could ask myself the question, "What exactly *is* the law of the Lord?" As I began to write a few words and see them on the page, as I worked with the images of tree and river, trying to draw close to what pleased and interested me about them, it occurred to me, the words suggested to me, that the "laws" of the physical universe could be considered as much the "law of the Lord" as the written words of the Scriptures regarding human behavior. Certainly they could be. They must be if we believe the physical universe is a manifestation of a creative power. The theme of the poem began to emerge. The "laws" of the physical world, those patterns of process put into words and mathematical language by scientists, are revealed by and are one with the objects that proclaim them. By "laws" I don't mean mandates or commandments formulated and delivered from outside the universe, but "laws" as the way that things are in nature, as the way the phenomena of the universe behave. These laws come into being simultaneously with the objects that embody and reveal them, in this instance trees. Here is the poem as it first appeared in my second book, *The Tattooed Lady in the Garden.*

HER DELIGHT
   After Psalm 1:2–3

The tupelo, the blackgum and the poplar,
The overcup oak and the water hickory stand
Along the riverbank being eternal law all day.
They have risen, transforming soil, yielding
To each other, spreading and bending in easy-sun
Contortions, just as their branches decreed they must
During their rising.

Their shadows cast shadow-law this evening
In the long narrow bars of steady black they make
Over the river, being the permanent mathematical
Matrixes they invent relative to the height
Of their ascending trunks.

And the law taking in the soft moisture
Of slow, pervading rivers underground
Is called root. And the root consistently sorting
Ion and mineral by the describable properties
Of its gated skin is called law.

The plum-shaped fruit of the tupelo
Is the rule defining the conformity
To which it shapes itself. The orange berry
Of the possumhaw creates the sugary orange law
Of the sun by which it makes its reality.
Every flattened pit and dark blue drupe and paper-skin
Seed obeys perfectly the commandment it fashions
By becoming itself.

The trees only write the eternal law
Of whatever they have written—the accomplishment
Of the blackgum ordaining autumn red
In the simultaneous commandment of its scarlet leaves;
The accomplishment of the hickory branching
Its leaf in naked, thin-veined everlasting statues
Of yellow across the sky.

And the woman standing this evening beneath the river trees,
Watching them rise by fissured bark, by husked and hardened
Fruit held high above the water, watching the long bodies
Of their shadows lying unmoved across the current,
She is the easy law that states she must become,
In the hazy, leaf-encroached columns of the evening sun,
Her meditation in this delight.

Only human beings are capable of delighting in these laws, both the processes and their descriptions, laws that simultaneously create the physical universe and are themselves created by the phenomena of the universe. Only human beings can recognize, celebrate, and delight in such "laws of the Lord," in the workings of the physical world. We and our delight are also part of that law. And only humans can meditate on their own delight. Perhaps this delight in meditation of the physical world is one element of righteousness.

I don't know whether the author of the first psalm had in mind the thought of my poem. Probably not. Perhaps generally he did, but certainly not explicitly. I imagine he had in mind by "law" the dictates governing human behavior that he believed were delivered to his people by God. However, it seems to me that the words of these verses are beautiful enough and suggestive enough, poetic enough, to have left open the possibility of other interpretations more suitable to the times and experiences of future generations, and to have left open that possibility without any loss of the original integrity of the verses. This may be wishful thinking on my part. It may also be mistaken and presumptuous.

The words "tree" or "trees" appear in the book of Psalms twelve times, almost always in positive connotations. However, in one instance, in Psalm 37:35, a wicked person is described as "spreading himself like a green bay tree." I suppose the suggestion is that a wicked person is boastful and arrogant and shallow. The following verse, verse 36, asserts that the wicked "passeth away and lo he was not." The green bay tree, I assume, experiences a similar fate. The green bay is not a flourishing tree and therefore provides an apt metaphor, in the mind of the psalmist, for a wicked person.

In Psalm 105, the poet recalls the plagues the Lord visited on the Egyptians during their refusal to release the Hebrews. Among frogs and caterpillars and "divers sorts of flies and lice" the Lord "gave them hail for rain and flaming fire in their land. / He smote their vines also and their fig trees; and brake the trees of their coasts" (Psalm 105:32–33). The destruction of forests and fig trees is given equal attention with raining hail and flaming fire and is listed along with turning "their waters into blood," slaying the fish, consuming all the herbs in the land, and devouring the fruit of the ground. This is a very angry God.

Trees, when mentioned in the Psalms, are most often symbols of the blessings of the Lord. They represent the health of the land. They are evidence of a bountiful earth given by a generous Lord. "The trees of the

Lord are full of sap; the cedars of Lebanon, which he hath planted; / Where the birds make their nests; as for the stork, the fir trees are her house" (Psalm 104:16–17). Trees, along with all aspects of the physical world, are called upon to praise the Lord. "Then shall all the trees of the wood rejoice / Before the Lord: for he cometh, for he cometh to judge the earth" (Psalm 96:12–13).

And again, as in Psalm 1, the righteous man is compared to a flourishing tree in Psalm 52:8 when the poet asserts, "But I am like a green olive tree in the house of God: I trust in the mercy of God for ever and ever." And in Psalm 92:12: "The righteous shall flourish like the palm tree: he shall grow like a cedar in Lebanon." Flourishing trees create and embody the "laws" of the earth governing growth, health, and fruitfulness. To the psalmist, they are evidence of a life in accordance with the earth and the laws of the Lord. "The earth is the Lord's and the fullness thereof" (Psalm 24:1). The majority of references to trees in the Psalms suggest that a vibrant, fruitful tree is a symbol of goodness, bounty, and a life that is right with the Lord. There is a definite affinity in the Psalms for comparing human beings and trees.

Can we become righteous and therefore a "flourishing tree" by study, by meditating on the glory of the physical universe, by engaging in those human disciplines that explore and celebrate the phenomena of life, the universe, and the "laws of the Lord" that are evident there? Can we create our souls in part through study and praise of the physical world, either through the arts or the sciences? And is this creative act in essence a spiritual act when it occurs? I don't know the answer to those questions, but the following are two poems which address them. Both were influenced by the images and themes contained in Psalm 1:2–3, though less directly influenced than "Her Delight." Words uttered by the artist van Gogh compose the title of this poem.

"THE TREE HAS CAPTURED MY SOUL"
    For Van Gogh

When they found him mad in the field
On his knees, gripping the hard wooden trunk
Of his own living soul, it could never be said

How it happened, whether the soul of the tree,
Its branches rising and interlocking like bones
Had disguised itself as skeleton and penetrated
The vision of his body that way undetected;
Or whether his soul willingly turned the vision of itself
Inside its own socket and became the pure white tree
Of its own interlocking; or whether he saw and testified
To the fragmentary parting of his soul caught
Among the wind and branches spreading across his canvas;
Or whether he captured his own body in the turning
Brushstrokes of a thousand yellow leaves and forfeited thereby
The treeless autonomy of his soul here on earth;
Or whether he lost the whole tree of his eye but gained
A vision of the veins of his soul rising and branching
Toward light; or whether the wind turned the soul
Of each yellow leaf inside its own socket
Until his eye was united everlastingly with that movement;
Or whether he saw the shimmering perception
Of that tree lift his body, light as a soul,
On the tips of its branches forever toward heaven.

But it is known that he came fully awake among them
In the field, his arms around his body
As if it were rooted in the earth, seeing
The illuminating wind of his soul for the first time
In all the possible movements of yellow
Each visionary leaf could offer him.

The following poem is more fanciful but also centers around the metaphor of human as tree and alludes to an important tree mentioned in Genesis. Sonia and Gordon, who appear in this poem, are two characters in the cast of characters in my book *Legendary Performance*.

DUALITY

Sonia says a single perfect tree lives inside her,
That the more she tries the more distinctly she can see it,
As if it stood alone on a hill against a light sky,
All the tangled details of its barks and girders and tapering
Twig crosses revealing themselves clearly. She says
She can examine the impetus in the brown, folded nubs
Of its new leaves if she wishes. She says the tree

Is stationary and multitudinous in her chest, untouched
And skeletal, almost like metal in its network against the sky.

And Sonia told Gordon the tree fills her body
Without pressure, its roots becoming one with her veins
And arteries. She can feel the small limber tips
Of its branches constantly in the palms of her hands.

She can detect, in her breath, the invention of its shifting
Attitude toward changing light. Anyone trained to look
With a scalpel could find its hardwood beginning in her brain.

Sonia says she wills the existence of the tree
By giving it a name, she wills the reality
Of the tree by giving it the location of her own body.
Sonia almost believes that the tree, created by the mind
But united with the body, can give the flesh eternity.

Gordon, laughing, calls it the Tree of Life.

As I was writing this essay, I happened to read an item posted on the Internet titled "Milwaukee Woman Sees Jesus in a Tree." The scene that I immediately imagined was of Jesus perched on a branch in a tree looking down at everyone, which seemed slightly humorous. However, it appears that Ella Huffin, sixty-three, one morning a week before Christmas, saw a figure of Jesus embodied in the trunk of an old tree in her yard. The article states, "Standing from a distance, at just the right angle, in an overcast day, the image is clear to Huffin. She said she sees Jesus looking down at a baby he's holding. . . . Visitors and Huffin never get tired staring at the image."[1] I mention this because it offers evidence once again that human as tree/ tree as human is an old story, an old and enduring metaphor present with us today. In whatever manner that metaphor might be configured or that story told, it almost always contains an element of the spiritual.

◆ ◆ ◆

The poem "Under the Big Top" begins with an epigraph taken from the well-known Twenty-third Psalm, "though I walk through the valley of the shadow." This poem is influenced by the following three verses in Psalm 23.

1 The Lord is my shepherd, I shall not want.
4 Yea, though I walk through the valley of the shadow of death, I shall fear no evil: for thou art with me: thy rod and thy staff they comfort me.
5 Thou preparest a table before me in the presence of mine enemies; thou anointest my head with oil; my cup runneth over.

In this poem, I wanted to adopt a slightly different approach to this famous psalm than is ordinarily taken. After all, our society is not so familiar with shepherds or with being anointed with oil, as the people at the time of David were. And many of us in this country may have a slightly different conception of enemies and God's relationship to the enemies of the "righteous" from that mentioned so often throughout the Psalms. Enemies appear in Psalm 23:5: "Thou preparest a table before me in the presence of mine enemies." A verse similar to the theme of Psalm 23 in this regard, though without its poetic power, appears in Psalm 138:7: "Though I walk in the midst of trouble, thou wilt revive me: thou shalt stretch forth thine hand against the wrath of mine enemies and thy right hand shall save me."

There is quite a bit of rhetoric throughout the book of the Psalms about "enemies," the "wicked," and the heathen, and many portrayals of God as a warrior-god, one who will destroy utterly the enemies of his faithful people. "Who is this King of glory? The Lord strong and mighty, the Lord mighty in battle" (Psalm 24:8). "For the Lord most high is terrible; he is a great King over all the earth. / He shall subdue the people under us, and the nations under our feet" (Psalm 47:2–3). Many of the psalms are prayers asking for help in conquering enemies. The voice in the psalms often expresses fear and anxiety. "Deliver me from mine enemies, O my God: defend me from them that rise up against me. / Deliver me from the workers of iniquity, and save me from bloody men.... Thou therefore, O Lord God of hosts, the God of Israel, awake to visit all the heathen: be not merciful to any wicked transgressors" (Psalm 59:1–2, 5). And again, "But thou, O God, shalt bring them down into the pit of destruction: bloody and deceitful men shall not live out half their days; but I will trust in thee" (Psalm 55:23). "O Babylon,

Babylon the destroyer, happy the man who repays you for all that you did to us! / Happy is he who shall seize your children and dash them against the rock" (Psalm 137:8–9; New English Bible).

I am disturbed by the sound and thrust of these words. I pull back, become distant and wary of the voice speaking. The poetry falters somewhat for me. I can imagine the circumstances that might give rise to these prayers, the fear and the anger, but the tone and the call for the abandonment of mercy, especially toward children, are disturbing to my contemporary mind and heart. However, echoes of this type of rhetoric, urging a God to annihilate an infidel enemy, remain today in many parts of the world.

Although the Lord as shepherd is a wonderful metaphor, one found in many books of the Bible, and we understand its implication, sheep herding is absent from the daily experiences of most of us. Thus this metaphor loses some of its original immediacy and impact for people today. In "Under the Big Top" I wanted to give a different, a contemporary setting to this thought of being comforted, protected, and accompanied through hard, dangerous, and frightening times in our lives. I wrote this rather whimsical poem for fun, just to see what might happen. Perhaps we could imagine being accompanied by the consoling, ministering spirits described in this poem, those "angels" putting on a bold front, a festive yet compassionate front, as humans often do.

UNDER THE BIG TOP
   ... though I walk through the valley of the shadow ...
   —Psalm 23

They're always here. One of them tumbles
in her maroon and silver-sequined tights before me,
as if she led, down the road. She somersaults, flips
mid-air over a hedge row, her bodice sparkling, over
a patch of butterfly pea. She does hand-stands
off curbs, cartwheels down alleys, leapfrogs
past parking meters. Crossing any bridge
with her is ceremony, a ritual of back bends
on thin wooden railings, toe-dances
on suspension cables.

How can I fear, one going ahead armed with chair
and fake pistol, two going ahead in epaulettes and brass
buttons, with marching drum, bold tasseled baton?

Another keeps a constant circle of blossoms
and pods spinning around my head. Tossing
and catching, he weaves almonds, apples, limes,
pomegranates, once the spotted eggs of the wood pewee,
once the buds of the Cherokee rose. So deft,
nothing he handles falls or shatters or bruises.
Even in the night far ahead I can see his torches,
their flames spiralling high into the black
dome, down again into his waiting hands.

And this one, such comfort, shuffles at my pace,
following one step behind. Holding his purple
pint-sized parasol above my head, he recovers
from each of his stumbles, tripping over stray dogs,
paper cups, raindrops, stepping on the dragging
cuffs of his own striped trousers. He keeps up,
guffawing when he hears me laugh, stopping abruptly
if I cease. And when he sees tears in my eyes,
he takes out his cowboy hankie, honks his schnoz,
presses two sad fingertips sincerely
to his garish grin.

Is this poem blasphemy? I don't consider it blasphemous. But I sup-
pose each reader must make that judgment. I don't believe that any
words or any written thoughts are sacrosanct, immune to questioning
or modification, not the words of the Bible and certainly not my own
words. I believe the Bible is the history of a people struggling within the
circumstances of their times to understand the questions that all great
art and literature and all honest religious thinkers struggle with. Where
did we come from? What is the meaning of human existence? What
are our obligations as conscious beings? Why do we die? What is the
source of our spiritual yearnings? What is the nature of the good life? I
can learn from the efforts of others to engage these questions, and I can
appreciate and benefit from their efforts. But I cannot rely upon them
conditionally, for then I risk forsaking my own time, the experiences and

insights and the resulting vision of my time, and my responsibilities to that vision.

✦ ✦ ✦

Both Psalm 1 and Psalm 23 are well-known and are often quoted. The sound of their words occupies a place in the psyche of our culture. I believe this is so because they are both fine, memorable poems, incorporating the artistic techniques that create and define lasting poetry—cadence and form, metaphor and repetition, subtlety, evocative imagery, coherence, a language of energy and integrity. These poetic techniques are found in many other psalms as well, but not all of them, in my opinion.

I believe poetry is essentially experiment with words and perceptions. One function of poetry, only one, is to question, to jostle and unsettle old entrenched ways of interpreting life and death in all their aspects. One function of poetry is to take an old, revered arrangement of words, an old music, and disassemble it, break it apart, not to destroy it and its ancient value but to reassemble it in new ways that might offer new perceptions, promote reassessment of long-held assumptions, create a new experience of the ordinary and the miraculous. Whether right or wrong, truthful or mistaken, successful or failing, I have written many poems attempting to broaden definitions of certain widely accepted concepts, "Angel of the Atom," "White Prayer," "The Answering of Prayers," "Good Heavens," "The Possible Suffering of a God During Creation," "Inside God's Eye," "Amen," and others.

Just as the poetry of the Psalms speaks first to the experiences of its time, any poetry must be intensely pertinent to its own moment before it can hope to possess pertinence within a wider context. I am grateful to have the words of the psalmist speaking to me, singing to me from long ago, from far back in recorded history, a voice from another place and another time providing a background for my attempts to express the human condition in my place and my time.

NOTES

1. TheMilwaukeeChannel.com, posted January 29, 2002.

PSALM 23

Catherine Sasanov

I was not raised with the Bible, much less with the Psalms, though we did have three copies of the Good Book in our house. The first was my Lutheran-gone-Presbyterian grandfather's copy, written in its lovely but inscrutable German script. My father may have been able to read it at one time, but his shaky hold on the paternal tongue had long since let go by the time I came into his life. The other two Bibles were also from my father's family, passed down from the Scots-Irish ancestors in the Missouri Ozarks. They were huge books, filled with pressed flowers, locks of hair, recipes for home remedies, advertisements for patent medicines, birth and death dates, and my great-great-uncle's impressions of the Battle of Wilson's Creek, one of the first battles of the Civil War, and how he went out to help bury the dead, pretty much in his own front yard. These books were less Bibles than oddly organized repositories of family history (go to First Corinthians for Aunt Maude's chestnut hair, the book of Revelation for the front page of the *Springfield Times* announcing the end of World War 1). There was never an inclination to turn even to the less fragile, less archival of the two books for spiritual guidance. We had priests for that. My mother's Irish-Catholic side won out in any discussion there may have been as to which faith my sisters and I would be raised in. Therefore, everything about the Bible, including the Psalms, was mediated through the priest I saw once a week and on holy days, always for an hour and usually when I wasn't listening. While I was very drawn to sacramentals (statues of saints, candles, incense, relics, rosaries, ashes, palms, bells, medals, and such), I was mostly bored silly with mass. Because of this, I set out on the road to retirement from the faith at age seven. I made what I thought was a complete break ten years later, once I was out of my mother's sight and had fled from one end of Illinois to the other to attend college. However, I have a sneaking suspicion that the saying is probably true: *Once a Catholic, always a Catholic.*

For all of my childhood distractions during mass (counting the crosses in church was usually how I passed my time) and years of general noninterest in religion, it amazes me that as an adult I find myself having the Twenty-third Psalm memorized start to finish in its King James entirety, completely by heart and without my having ever intended to learn it. But perhaps that's the secret: *I learned it by heart.* Not by assignment, catechism, or other kind of coercion. Little by little, death by death, wake by wake. From the antique bookmark I found in a secondhand shop. From the back of the laminated obituary marking my mother's passing. On the flyers handed out by silent women in front of the ruins of the World Trade Center. I hear its echoes in Coolio's song "Gangsta's Paradise"—"As I walk through the valley of the shadow of death / I take a look at my life and realize there's nothing left . . ."—and in Thomas Merton's prayer from *Thoughts in Solitude*: "My Lord God . . . I trust you always, though I seem to be lost and in the shadow of death. I will not fear for you are ever with me. . . ." It is subverted in Lucia Perillo's poem "For a Catholic Girl": "*Though I'm racing my ass through the shadow of some god/damned valley I fear . . . blah blah, blah blah . . . no death . . .*" Lord knows where else I came across it. In short stories, novels, movies, probably with only the first lines recited to set a graveside scene. And I must have heard it in church, when it wheeled its way around in the cycle of responsorial Psalms during mass, all of which I recall being so dull and uninspired, it was years before I associated them with the Psalms in the Bible.

Being Catholic, my family's parish never used the King James version that I had somehow memorized, though it seemed to sneak in from time to time on the back of memorial cards at funerals. In recent years, when I've found myself in churches a bit more frequently and listening a lot harder, what I have heard are translations of Psalm 23 that are dumbed down and flattened out; like many of the psalms, they've had so much mystery, ambiguity, and powerful imagery worked out of them, the poet in me wants to run screaming from my pew. I barely recognize these versions for the psalm I picked up mostly on the street and in the presence of the dead. The translations read as if they were constructed by committee and through consensus, without poet or Holy Spirit anywhere in sight. Whoever they were (and in the case of the New American Bible, it was fifty Bible scholars) the group kept the windows not only tightly locked against letting that bird into the room, but with the curtains drawn so they wouldn't have to see it beating its wings against the glass.

A number of these translations were made in the 1960s and 1970s, in the wake of changes that came to Catholicism after Vatican II. In opening the church up to the needs of the faithful in the twentieth century, many changes were long needed and appreciated. Those that were more regrettable were almost always brought on by someone's extreme interpretation of one point or another in the Vatican II documents. I don't think it's coincidental that during this period when stripped-down, plainspoken versions of the psalms appeared, a stripping away and/or sanitizing of church imagery and devotional objects was also taking place. Many churches around the country experienced the same wholesale housecleaning our parish saw: Saints being hustled out statue by statue, clearing the place of the usual suspects one contemplated, looked up to, or asked intercession from. Relic cases, with their assortment of saintly bone fragments, hair strands, and clothing shreds, all of which were lent out from time to time to the sick, disappeared as well. New crucifixes were installed over many altars, but frequently Christ was almost unrecognizable from the wood he was nailed on. Joseph and Mary were often the only other figures added to a sanctuary. In St. Bridget's they stood on either side of the altar with cool, distant expressions that matched the temperature of their dazzlingly white marble skin. In many parishes, what was mysterious and sensual receded into the past. No more the smell of wax and water. Candles disappeared, and often incense as well. Altar boys were told to stop ringing the bells that announced the consecration of the body and blood. Twenty years after they were first silenced, I would find myself continuing to hear a phantom ringing in my head during particular moments in the mass. It reminded me of how some amputees continue to feel the limbs they lost in a distant war or accident. In many churches, all signs of psychic or physical suffering were also banished. Statues of Our Lady of Sorrows were often replaced by more upbeat images of the Virgin Mother. There was no more evidence, much less talk, of anything as visceral as the Precious Blood, the Five Wounds, the Shoulder Wound, the Blood Sweat, the Agony in the Garden, the Scourging, or the Crown of Thorns. Jesus went from crèche to Christ without a scratch, the cross appearing more trampoline than torture chamber to propel him on his way.

Disconcerting as all this was for many Catholics, it was usually well-intentioned. There was a real concern in the church that parishioners were paying less attention to the Gospels than they were to sacramentals and rituals that, taken too far, bordered on the talismanic and superstitious. (One of the more extreme examples was the use of super-short, ejaculatory prayers which, if repeated a certain number of times, earned one indulgences from the church.) Some of the devout thought that all that was needed to be a really good Catholic, besides going to mass, was to surround oneself with devotional objects and take part in their attendant prayers and rituals. Other ways of acting out Christ's teachings in their lives were sometimes lost in these more meditative activities.

But instead of reminding their congregations of the deeper meaning of devotional objects, prayers, and rituals, then adapting them to enliven the more prosaic aspects of the faith, many parishes just did away with them entirely. Whether it was true or not, the sweeping out and/or sanitizing of these items, as well as the dumbing down of language in Psalms and other religious texts, appeared to have arisen out of a concern among church hierarchy that Catholics *just didn't get it*. There was too much *stuff* (relics, statues, candles, incense, bells, blood) distracting the faithful from the Good News. As for the Good News, the striving for plainspokenness and clarity that came with the all-inclusive language movement stripped many of the psalms and other scripture of exactly the kind of language that made them memorable. In both the temple and the text, what was most evocative, multilayered in meaning, and making use of poetic devices (metaphor, simile, image, symbol) was what found itself most frequently rooted out.

Perhaps some of the discomfort came from the fact that poetry, whether it is that in the language of the Psalms or the poetry imbued in particular objects and devotions of the church, isn't built for linear thinking. Catholics live with imagery, sometimes puzzle over it, but often coexist peacefully with its mysteries even when they are not completely understood or when the understanding comes first to the heart as opposed to the head. An example of this would be the deep peace that comes in uniting one's prayer with the lighting of a candle, whether or not one consciously knows that the rising smoke symbolizes the raising of prayer to Heaven or that its light provides a literal and symbolic stay against darkness. The act becomes ritual, focusing the person in their prayer and reinforcing the moment through their senses (the scent of wax, the flame's heat, the sputter of the candles, the fire's dance in response to the breeze set in motion by a passerby or the opening of a door).

This particular act loses much in the compromise some churches have made with their parishioners by providing electric candles. These are set up in rows on stands, much as candles were in the past. But that is where the similarity ends. The candleholders themselves are plastic, lidded, and often sheathed in open-ended glass cylinders that can be slipped on and off. The glass is made thick, red, and opaque to obscure just how much the "candles" inside them look exactly like toilet paper rolls with a light-bulb on top. Wire is run through each one of these off-white plastic tubes to connect with the small bulb. Once the stand is plugged in and money is deposited into it, one lights the candle by pushing a button located on its lid. A small, nervous flickering appears as electricity surges through the bulb's filaments while the murky red plastic and glass do their best to conceal the fact that there is no flame. The symbolism of prayer raised to Heaven on a candle's smoke is completely lost here. (For that matter, there would be something seriously wrong if there *was* smoke.) If one of the reasons candles disappeared from churches was because priests felt that parishioners didn't understand the symbolism of lighting them, electric candles do little or nothing to clarify that deeper significance. Lighting one has all the attendant mystery of turning on any household appliance. It does little to appeal to the emotions, much less the senses. Basically, it just gets the job done. I find the advertising for these candles in the Jesuit weekly *America* quite telling: "Electric candles. Why? Profitable, Safe, Clean, Devotional, Zero Maintenance, *Profitable!*" For the manufacturer, and also for the buyer attracted to this ad, it appears that deepening a congregation's devotional life certainly isn't the priority.

If I have lingered with my comparison between wax and electric candles, it's because I don't think it is too far afield from a comparison of the translations of Psalm 23 as they are found in the King James version (KJV) and the New American Bible (NAB), the second of which is published by the U.S. Conference of Catholic Bishops. I will go over only a few of the more significant wording differences between their respective versions, but I think they are example enough of the poetic versus the more prosaic translation. In each of the following cases, the King James version is first, with the New American Bible version following (and I am working from the most recent edition of the NAB, 1991):

> Yea, though I walk through the valley of the shadow of death . . .
> Even when I walk through a dark valley . . .

> He restoreth my soul.
> You restore my strength.

> I will dwell in the house of the LORD forever.
> I will dwell in the house of the LORD for years to come.

A footnote to the NAB version of the Twenty-third Psalm says that "a different division of the Hebrew consonants yields the translation 'the valley of the shadow of death.'" It doesn't say, however, whether that reading is wrong. Was "in the valley of the shadow of death" just a fortunate accident of mistranslation? After all, what darker valley is there than *that*? Or was the Hebrew made to be ambiguous? Poets often see ambiguity as a gift to be grateful for, not a problem to be solved. The original Hebrew may have allowed for the idea that the Lord could accompany the supplicant in both the most mundane and the most supernaturally treacherous kinds of darkness. Translation being what it is, the English language limits the choice to one image or the other. But why go with the weaker, less evocative of the two? A "dark valley" most of us can probably maneuver with a strong heart, a good flashlight, and a map. The "valley of the shadow of death" is a whole different matter. The intensity of this image and the way it rolls off the tongue make it one of the best-known lines of any in Psalms.

"He restoreth my soul / You restore my strength." *Soul* or *strength*: Which is closer to the Hebrew text? *Soul* is certainly the more evocative of the two words. With rest, dietary supplements, exercise, and a doctor's good advice, one could probably restore their strength pretty much on their own. But to restore one's *soul*—that is a kind of strength obtained, at least in part, with divine assistance. And the restoration of strength in general is implied in the soul's refurbishing.

Finally, "I will dwell in the house of the LORD . . ." If I had a choice of having goodness and mercy by dwelling in the house of the LORD *forever* as opposed to having goodness and love by dwelling in the house of the Lord *for years to come*, I'd go with the former. The latter sounds like my tenancy will be up at some point. Why rent when you can buy? As for *forever*: Forever is too long in some places, but perhaps not in paradise.

Is the reader done a disservice when the striving for clarity and plainspokenness irons out what is complex and evocative from Psalms and other religious texts? The NAB version is clear, but prosaic in the extreme. Perhaps it is more faithful to the Hebrew than the King James or the countless other translations of the Twenty-third Psalm that have been made over time. I don't know. What I do know is that the King James is the version most people seem to know or are drawn to, whether it was used in their church or not. For some people this might be a matter of nostalgia, of having grown up with that translation. But I think it is more than that. I think the attraction to the King James version will always be due to the power of its metaphor and imagery, as well as the fact that it *doesn't* read like modern-day vernacular English. It doesn't sound like something someone might spout off on the street corner while waiting for the bus. Its slightly archaic diction is mysterious and formal, setting it apart from the mundanities of this world. While I think people love the idea of clarity, I don't think most people want the Psalms to read like their local newspaper.

The pity is that the New American Bible *did* have a version of Psalm 23 (from the NAB's first edition, published in 1970) that wasn't too bad. With some tweaking, it could have given the King James a run for its money. In the 1970 version, one can hear the translator truly striving toward a poetic rendering of the work. Some rhyme (repose/soul; foes/ overflows) is made use of, emphasizing long vowel sounds that accentuate the psalm's almost languid calm. And the word choice is lush: pastures are "verdant," waters "restful," the soul "refreshed." In this version, the translator's word choice also better fits the psalm's overall meaning. For example, there is a big difference between "only goodness and kindness *follow* me" (NAB version, 1970) and "only goodness and love *pursue* me" (NAB version, 1991). While "pursue" is perhaps the more interesting of the two verbs, there isn't any wandering off, much less running away, by the speaker in Psalm 23 to prompt its use. However, in both NAB versions of the psalm one finds the more mundane "dark valley" as opposed to the King James's more evocative "valley of the shadow of death." Both versions also end with dwelling in the house of the Lord "for years to come" as opposed to the more powerful "I will dwell in the house of the LORD forever" that one finds in the King James.

In comparing the NAB's 1970 and 1991 versions, one can imagine the conversation that must have taken place between those revisionists who felt that the 1970 text wasn't clear enough for readers: "*Verdant?* Who came up with *verdant?* How about *green* pastures? Everyone knows what a *green* pasture looks like." The NAB's 1970 translation, "In verdant pastures he gives me repose," comes close to the beauty of the KJV line, "He maketh me to lie down in green pastures." But what the reader ends up with is the NAB's 1991 revision, "In green pastures you let me graze." The line is not only rhythmically flat but also pushes the peopleas-sheep metaphor way too far and in the wrong direction. At least in the NAB's earlier version, there was trust on the part of the translator that the reader would be intelligent enough to puzzle out the meaning of "verdant" within the context of the rest of the poem.

Sound and rhythm apparently were the last thing on the translator's mind for the 1991 version; his or her goal appears to have been clarity at all cost, sacrificing any music that might make the psalm evocative and memorable. How someone thought that going from "The LORD is my shepherd; I shall not want" (found both in the KJV and in the NAB's 1970 translation) to "The Lord is my shepherd; there is nothing I lack" would represent an improvement is beyond me. All I can figure is that the translator wanted to separate his or her version as much as possible from the King James translation. The sad part of using a word like "lack" is that there is a harshness in its consonant and vowel sounds that works aurally against the psalm's idea of gentleness, peace, and calm. Also, "There is nothing I lack" implies an external need for provisions being met, whereas "I shall not want" suggests the idea of an inner longing being satisfied.

The attention given to the smallest details of language and sound is what makes for evocative writing, especially poetry. Poetry is the form we so often turn to as writers or readers when our hearts are broken, when we grieve, when we are afraid. There is something about poetry that is a vessel ready-made for holding our hearts. Psalm 23 is a poem, a song of trust, a belief that no matter how terrible one's enemies, no matter how fearful the path, in life and death we will be remembered, loved, and watched over for all time. In the multitude of interviews taped after 9/11, one man held it together pretty well while recalling the story of his escape from one of the two World Trade Center towers. He broke down completely, though, during his recollection of how people working their way down the stairwells began to spontaneously recite the Twenty-third Psalm together. It wasn't lost on him—nor, would I think, was it lost on much of the TV audience—that this prayer of trust so associated with the dead had been recited by people who knew they were praying over what might end up being their own corpses.

Even though Psalm 23 is not a psalm about suffering, it is rooted in the Catholic need to trust that Christ will be there in times of physical, mental, emotional, and spiritual brokenness. The need at times for an assistance beyond all human help is one reason people turn to Psalm 23. In his book *Redemptive Suffering*, William J. O'Malley writes that "in Jesus, God became suffering. . . . In Jesus, God felt death." Because Christ went through his own personal experience with human terror, humiliation, and grief, he appears as the shepherd who will come to each individual with deep empathy for the depth and range of their sorrows.

As I mentioned earlier in this essay, churches that did away with much of their devotional imagery and rituals also often eradicated any imagery that smacked of suffering. The image of a crucified Christ is absent from many churches, along with those of Our Lady of Sorrows and Our Lady of Solitude. It's not unusual that Christ is often solely figured as the risen Lord, while the cross above the altar is either bare or embellished with a Christ that is nearly indistinguishable from the cross's wood. Images of Christ's suffering, and of his mother's grief at losing her child, can be discomforting to look at, but they are a crucial part of the whole redemption story. I wonder whether their absence, consciously or not, comes in part from our society's belief that suffering has no redeeming qualities whatsoever and is to be avoided at all costs. The problem is that no matter what therapies, drugs, medical procedures, self-help books, or investment plans Americans gather to themselves, suffering still finds us. While churches don't need to wallow in the imagery, I wonder if its absence doesn't cheat parishioners out of not just a visual reminder that Christ suffered in his human body, mind, and heart as they also suffer, but that it robs parishioners of a contemplative focal point as well. A personal story illustrates this: One of my most vivid memories as a child was when my mother brought a small crucifix to the local priest to have it blessed. While the cross had a fairly realistic-looking, suffering Jesus nailed onto it, I don't remember the overall effect to be gruesome. But when my mother took it out of its tissue paper and passed it to the priest, he promptly gave it back to her, saying, "Oh, Peggy, we don't bless things like this anymore!"

In devotional text, there was once incredible imagery and metaphor around the wounded body of Christ that is mostly absent now from contemporary prayer. The idea of fleeing into Christ's wounds when pursued by evil, putting a drop of Christ's Precious Blood on one's heart to find resolve and strength, or slipping one's desires into the side wound of Jesus so he can hold them in his heart—all of these spectacular images from what are now mostly unused prayers redeem the Lord's butchered body and turn it into fortress, fountain, and strongbox. Through such imagery the body takes on multiple layers of meaning and utility.

As the church is a sacred space, with ambiance and objects that reinforce it as a place in the world, yet set apart, the same can be said for the Psalms. Their beauty comes, like that of all good poems, in that there is often an understanding in the heart before a complete intellectual comprehension. And when intellectual comprehension does come, the Psalms may open onto layered meanings, not just one interpretation. These meanings often take on subtle changes or open out into revelation as the reader grows older and returns to the text, bringing his or her life experience to the words.

I wonder if there would be less need to remove or flatten out the more metaphoric or multilayered church texts if there was a deeper discussion of them within the church itself. Instead of distracting or stumping us, imagery, metaphor, simile, and symbol can all add to an enrichment of one's faith. This goes as well for those objects and devotional items that were removed from or sanitized by many churches. These items can focus us, pull us deeper into the faith through sensuality and ritual. Sacramentals don't make a church—its people do—but the richness of poetry, and the power of devotionals and their attendant rituals, have the ability to enliven the spiritual life. I think of all the churches in New York, Boston, and other cities and towns on 9/11, where if people could find candles, whether electric or wax, they lit them. Others brought them to street corners, to firehouses, to the Brooklyn promenade, to parks, to gatherings. They were a visual version of Psalm 23, these thousands of small lights lit against what surely seemed in those early days like the darkness of the valley of the shadow of death. Prayers rising on smoke from people shaken and suffering, but hopeful that goodness and mercy would follow the dead and the living, not just for years to come, but forever.

I SHALL NOT WANT
The Twenty-third Psalm Comes to Cleveland, Ohio

David Citino

A Psalm of David

1   The Lord is my shepherd; I shall not want.
2   He maketh me to lie down in green pastures: he leadeth me beside the still waters.
3   He restoreth my soul: he leadeth me in the paths of righteousness for his name's sake.
4   Yea, though I walk through the valley of the shadow of death, I will fear no evil: for thou art with me; thy rod and thy staff they comfort me.
5   Thou preparest a table before me in the presence of mine enemies: thou anointest my head with oil; my cup runneth over.
6   Surely goodness and mercy shall follow me all the days of my life: and I will dwell in the house of the Lord forever.

Perhaps the best-known six verses of the Hebrew Bible and the Christian, this ageless psalm has depicted down through the ages an essential perceived relationship between humans young and old and their God. The creator of heaven and earth, man and woman, the inventor of diverse languages, the boat-designer and rain-maker, the one who nailed down the covenant deal, the dynasty builder, plague-maker and law-giver, the bloodthirsty warrior-god of Joshua and Judges has evolved now into the shepherd, whose followers are sheep. The symbology of shepherd and sheep in intimate relationship runs throughout Judaism and Christianity.

It's not surprising that an agrarian nation's writers would find poetry and music in the pasture, that is, out of an ancient and important source of food and clothing. Other passages of the Bible make the same ovine analogy, for example, Ezekiel 34:14: "I will feed them in good pasture, and upon the high mountains of Israel shall their fold be; there shall they lie in a good fold, and in a fat pasture shall they feed upon the mountains of Israel." Rapturous about his blushing bride, the bridegroom of the Song of Solomon tells her, "Thy two breasts are like two young roes that are twins, which feed among the lilies." He employs sheep to help him praise the fact that she still has all her teeth: "Thy teeth are like a flock of sheep which came up from the washing; whereof every one bears twins, and none is barren among them." At the Jordan River, John the Baptist looks up at the approaching Jesus and says to all, "Behold the Lamb of God!" (John 1:36). Adam names all the critters God had made early in Genesis:

> And whatsoever Adam called every living creature,
> that was the name thereof. And Adam gave names to all cattle,
> and to the fowl of the air, and to every beast of the field.

Animals were seen as magical fellow-creatures, big-eyed and gentle or fierce and fanged totems of the tribes.

While naming the animals, Adam actually is looking for a love, a "help meet" companion to last a lifetime. When the aardvark and weasel and wapiti prove unsuitable, God creates Eve from Adam's rib. Noah fills his ark with two (or seven, depending on the strand woven into the narrative) kinds of every animal, illustrating that we all, humans and beasts, were, and I would argue still are, in the same boat. Samson murders a lion with his bare hands, and "the bees made honey in the lion's head" (as the passage in Judges and the old spiritual tell us). He uses the jawbone of an ass to slay a thousand Philistines. Jesus speaks of a camel passing through the eye of a needle and the birds of the air, and rides into Jerusalem on an ass he has his disciples get for him in a designated place. The books of Daniel in what Christians call the Old Testament, and Revelation in the New, are full of fantastical beasts that roar, fume, wriggle, and fly.

I used to envy my country-dwelling cousins who kept a large herd of Black Angus cattle, raised sheep and chickens, and entered 4-H and Future Farmers of America competitions each year. I traveled from the city to help them get in the hay each summer, and suffered asthma attacks each July. I was convinced that they could better understand a psalm about sheep, or a stable in which "the cattle are lowing, the poor baby wakes" and where "the ass and the ox kept time," all part of a religion that used animals for bloody sacrifice to the God who made them but also unearthly singing of God's praise. The loud, cavernous barn outside Medina, Ohio, erected by Amish carpenters, took my breath away; but I could see there a life closer to the Bible than the life I was experiencing on the west side of Cleveland (although I knew well there was a slaughterhouse in operation not too far from my home that announced itself, especially on summer nights, with a rank, ungodly aroma that lifted over the neighborhood like a siren). This is what God wants from his worshippers, lots of bawling, shitting beasts, the stink of charred flesh, oxen after oxen, dove by dove? This pleases him? I found that puzzling, even then.

It's important to remember that the psalms are songs; we've lost the original music, but we have the lyrics—at least translations of translations of the lyrics. The Hebrew title of this book is *Hallel*, "praise," and while most of the songs praise God and describe the majesty of the Almighty, nearly all include as well the singer's sense of self as part of a very human lament. *This is how great God is, and this (sadly) is who we are*, each song in the Book of Psalms announces. Shepherd and sheep, for example.

Scholars tell us that the words "A Psalm of David," like the other superscriptions of the Book of Psalms, were added by the rabbis who copied the Hebrew and then the Jewish texts (translations of the Hebrew scripture into other languages for non-Hebrew-speaking Jews). Also added by the rabbis were the *Amen* and *Selah* that appear in some Bible translations. The former is an opportunity for the congregation to give assent to what has been sung. *Amen* allows the audience to say, "You said it!" *Selah* is something of a mystery. I favor the view that the word announces a musical interlude to the singing. In the Bible as Literature course I teach I liken *selah* to "Hit it, boys," or even "Break it down for me, fellas."

While the attribution to David of so many of the psalms may not help us understand any particular one, it certainly helps us appreciate the ways later generations revered—and, of course, heard—these "Greatest Hits" from "the singer of Israel's songs." These songs are great because David wrote and sang them. David is great because he wrote the psalms. I used to say to my Bible students that another title for the Book of Psalms could be "The Boss's Greatest Hits," but with history marching on, as it does, too few of my undergraduate students know Bruce Springsteen, and I've had to quit using the line. At any rate, Israel's holy songbook has been seen as the product of the genius of David, Israel's greatest king and the individual many Christians claim was the ancestor of Jesus himself.

The plain diction and simplicity of the Twenty-third Psalm put me in mind of Blake's Songs of Innocence, but there is a certain darkness within these seemingly childlike lines. (Blake's innocence too contains such shadows, of course.) These complexities are not always pointed out by religious instructors of the young, who probably couldn't understand that children and the old are the real believers.

I remember vividly the religious songs of my childhood, and the chills they'd engender up and down the spine, the hairs on the back of my neck standing up as the organ roared,

Jesus loves me, this I know,
'Cause the Bible tells me so.
Little ones to him belong:
They are weak but he is strong.

Yes, we are weak—defenseless little sheep—and he is the adult, the all-knowing sheepherder. "He's got the whole world in his hands, / He's got the whole wide world in his hands," and "Jesus wants me for a sunbeam, sunbeam, a sunbeam."

I was raised Roman Catholic, and singing wasn't as important to me as it seemed to be to my Protestant sisters and brothers. Also, there were songs I couldn't sing along with them. (The martial strains of "A Mighty Fortress Is Our God" became permissible only after the ecumenical spirit of Vatican II.) For their part, the Protestant boys and girls wouldn't sing along with me, because several of my songs were directed not to the shepherd but to his mother. As a Catholic, especially because I inherited the garlic-scented Mediterranean variety with its ingrained, ancient Mariolatry—the Virgin's brilliant blue veil and dolorous eyes—I sang not to God or Jesus but to the Queen of Heaven:

> On this day, O beautiful mother,
> On this day we give thee our love.
> Near thee, Madonna, fondly we hover,
> Trusting thy gentle care to prove.

So much of religious education involves adults teaching children to sing to high heaven and to do so in performances to the same adults.

Another special song we sang on the birthday celebration of our pastor at Ascension of Our Lord School in Cleveland. (It was later, in Latin class at St. Ignatius High School, that I'd learn that *pastor* is Latin for "shepherd." The Twenty-third Psalm made even more sense to me then.) My pastor's song, which all eight grades practiced in the church during the day for two weeks before the big day—squirming pews patrolled by sharp-eyed nuns with chirping clickers in their hands, rosaries at their sides—I've never had the courage to forget:

> Ask dear Mother Mary to shield him,
> Till his years in thy service shall cease.
> Dear Heart of Jesus hear our prayer,
> Please take our pastor 'neath thy care.

It seemed to me, from the defeated air, the look of the scored face and hands, and the shock of white hair, that for the dour old man, the particular shepherd to whom we sang, whose breath always smelled of cheap wine from the stash in the sacristy, the years were very close to ceasing. At least when they did, he finally could quit having to worry and preach so many sermons about money and the building fund.

In second grade I learned other songs—the Latin answers of the mass. That is, I memorized the sounds of the responses, strange-tasting syllables of a language not dead to me because it was not yet born. I knew it sounded little like the only other foreign language I knew anything about, the musical Calabrian dialect of Italian my grandparents sang in their fragrant kitchen and garden, though the priest's Latin and their sibilant peasant syllables both were tinted with the nasal accents of the Diocese of Cleveland. At the beginning of the mass, the priest would intone, *Introibo ad altare Dei* ("I will go up to the altar of God . . ."), and I'd answer, like a doo-wop backup singer dancing behind the lead, *Ad Deum qui laetificat juventutem maum* (". . . to God who gives joy to my youth"). "Joy" was inaccurate, really. This strange music frightened the boy dressed in black cassock and white surplice kneeling beside the priest at the foot of the altar. This was serious, soulful music. Here was a child who each night in bed uttered a somber prayer: "If I should die before I wake, please take me to heaven." One false step, one wrong word, and he could face both earthly and unearthly wrath.

During the rite of Benediction—for which, as a seventh- and eighth-grade altar boy, I'd carry the gaudy gold-plate monstrance with the large disc of the unleavened body of God pressed behind the glass—we sang those late-Latin hit tunes, *Tantum ergo* and *O Solutaris, hostia,* which in the room of my skull throughout the day and in my dreams competed with Buddy Holly,

> I had a girl, Donna was her name.
> Since she's left me, I've never been the same.

Skeeter Davis sang of love directed not at God or his mother or Communion of Saints but at a boy who, perhaps, sat next to her in school. Still, this was an all-encompassing passion:

> To know, know, know him
> Is to love, love, love him,
> Just to see him smile
> Makes my life worthwhile
> To know, know, know him
> Is to love, love, love him,
> And I do.

The line dividing songs to natural lovers from songs to supernatural and preternatural ones was indistinct in those fervid days. Weren't mothers on earth representatives of the Mother of God? They would have wisdom to share with their sons and daughters:

> When I was just a little boy, I asked my mother,
> What would I be?
> Would I be handsome, would I be rich?
> Here's what she said to me.
> *Que sera, sera.* Whatever will be, will be.
> The future's not ours to see.
> *Que sera, sera.*

What perfect wisdom—the sort of eloquence imparted to a child by a parent that can last a lifetime. And Ferlin Husky gave a particular vision of the end of Noah's flood and perhaps Pentecost as well:

> On the wings of a snow-white dove,
> He sends his pure sweet love,
> A sign from above
> On the wings of a dove.

And one of the most successful and powerful earthly psalmists of my youth was known as the King. He asked, in song, a classic, existential human question,

> Ah well-a bless my soul what's wrong with me?
> I'm itchin' like a man on a fuzzy tree.

They don't write similes like that anymore, by God!—especially ones introduced by a blessing referencing the questioner's own immortal soul. Every preteen and teen knows that itching and yearning. A fuzzy tree! The Tree of the Knowledge of Good and Evil, back in the garden, perhaps? The old rugged cross itself? Buddy, Skeeter, and Elvis and the host of their crooning, wailing, moony tribe on *American Bandstand* and popular radio were psalmists of a new religion in my life then. This was a world of girls with twirling skirts, bobby sox, and budding blouses nothing like the dark impenetrable habits of the Religious Sisters of Mercy. These secular psalms shook me up, rocked my soul back then, just as the God-music did, the Gregorian chants, the abject praises and pleas, hymn after hymn. They all play in my head, competing even today.

While on the one hand the Twenty-third Psalm can be experienced as the "Twinkle, Twinkle, Little Star" of religious teaching, conjuring as it does a child's wonder-world of magic, total dependence, and total trust—and a fable in which an animal can speak to God on behalf of other animals—still there is some heavier, adult matter between the notes and words.

By means of the declarative statement at the outset, the speaker announces the metaphoric realities of the relationship between God and self.

The Lord = the shepherd.
I = a sheep.

The shepherd's job is to protect the sheep from predators, starvation, thirst, and treacherous territory, among other dangers. There are wolves—some of them disguised in sheep's clothing—patrolling the night. There are pools of bad water, ditches, and poison weeds. Ill omens loom everywhere, and always there is the potential for bad weather. The tools of the master's trade are the "rod" and "staff," the curved crook and stout walking stick, which, by the way, remain the symbolic tools of the bishop even today. The shepherd can beat back a predator or grab my neck with his crook to prevent me from falling.

We sheep need constant protection, of course, so meek and mild, lacking in assertiveness and defenses are we, the epitome of innocent victims. We move about with eyes down on the ground most of the time, while the shepherd has two long legs and the ability to see and know things we can't—our destiny, for starters. We're bound for altar or table, rendering place or mill. Moreover, the implication is that while there are multiple shepherds and multiple sheep, "The Lord" and no other is ours. Because of the skill and power of this shepherd, "I shall not want," the speaker/sheep claims—the implication being that sheep of other shepherds may indeed have wants and needs. A shepherd who can provide the end to all wanting is powerful indeed. Omnipotent, even. We sheep want and want; above all we desire that the shepherd make us stop wanting. Here we have not the key to all mythology, but at least the heart of so much religious experience and so many prayers: I want many things, but above all else, I want to stop having to want.

The psalmist follows with an enumeration of some of the ways this particular shepherd provides for his sheep. In an arid land where grassy leas and potable water are scarce, his gifts of "green pastures" and "still waters" are most welcome and most valuable. I've always found fascinating the two ways of reading "He maketh me to lie down." He creates me (just) so that I can do this, and/or he orders me to lie down, and the result is as life-sustaining as it is pleasurable.

The language swerves from one side of the metaphor to the other at this point. We understand better now the poetical parallelism that is, according to Robert Alter (in *The Art of Biblical Poetry*), the defining mark of Hebrew poetry. "Restoreth my soul" is linked synonymously to "green pastures," and the "still waters" he "leadeth me beside" exist in parallel with "the paths of righteousness for his name's sake" that "he leadeth me to." While parables are closed narratives, at least until the teacher explains their application to this world, many of the psalms jump from tenor to vehicle, the other world to this one, green pastures of paths of righteousness, and back again.

The psalmist breaks out in an interjection or sudden, brief prayer— what we called years back, for reasons no eighth-grade boy or girl could fathom, an "ejaculation." We said, "My Lord and my God," or "Jesus, Mary, and Joseph." The psalmist raises her or his voice and sings "Yea." Yes, verily! Oh, man! Wow! Even were the speaker "to walk through the valley of the shadow of death" (what a spooky place a child or an adult can imagine this to be, though this particular sheep is not there yet, apparently), "I will fear no evil: for thou art with me." The shepherd is carrying the tools of his trade, the weapons and marks of authority, "thy rod and thy staff" that "comfort me."

It's interesting that the "yea" marks a sudden shift from third person to second. The shepherd is now addressed by the sheep as "thou." No longer "I and God," the speaker has achieved the "I and thee" relationship that Martin Buber wrote about. It's almost as if the emotions, the abject "wants" of the singer, and the heightened state to which the song brings him or her provoke an outburst, a cry from the heart. As Balaam's eloquent ass did after seeing an angel, a sheep can break out of character in the face of extraordinary duress and speak truth.

The second-person dialogue continues. Not only does the shepherd prepare "a table before me," he does so "in the presence of mine enemies." It's one thing to be given a sumptuous meal; it's even sweeter to be able to sit down to eat where one's worst enemies must witness the feasting (without being able themselves to eat). You don't just vanquish my foes, Lord, the sheep says. You let me eat in front of them. (And while every child knows it's not polite to eat in front of someone else, well, if God gives permission then it must be all right.) What's more, "thou anointest my head with oil." You treat me like a king, pouring out oil the way the kings of Israel were anointed by the prophets. I'm the most honored guest at the feast.

The first line of this psalm is known everywhere. So too is the all-encompassing metaphor we encounter at this point, the culmination of the water imagery and of the argument of the entire poem: "My cup runneth over." You know, shepherd: even in this land of dust and thirst, you more than give me drink. You pour out so much of the water or wine (or both) that it breaks the meniscus of the surface and runs down the sides of the cup—and of course my thirsty, hungry enemies have to watch this wasteful beneficence, too.

This song has been popular on a mythic level for so many centuries for a number of reasons. It explores in the language of children, and the language of the child persisting in every adult, the relationship humans imagine exists between them and the God who they believe leads them to the next pasture with his rod and staff. They can conceive of their God as a loving, watchful shepherd. The song is a prayer of praise to this deity, but it also reminds him that his sheep are depending on him totally for the most basic needs—food, water, protection from predators; and right now the shepherd seems not to be doing all he could for his charges, else there would be no need for such a psalm. So many of the psalms are gentle reminders to God, pushes, pulls, and tugs at the divine conscience, lyrical requests to him to get busy.

"Surely," the sheep-singer concludes, "goodness and mercy shall fol-
low me all the days of my life: and I will dwell in the house of the Lord
forever." "Surely"? This seems a weak, even a prevaricating intensifier.
"Surely you don't think goodness and mercy *won't* follow," the implica-
tion seems to be. "Surely it *won't* happen (will it?) that I ever will leave
the Lord's house?!" Perhaps sheep realize that, whatever happens from
pasture to pasture, even if they can briefly cease being sheep and speak
up directly to the shepherd, still they are powerless, ultimately, to fend
and provide for themselves when the song ends and the music drifts
away.

WANT

Angie Estes

> What if loss and desire
> were not a split curtain
> ever parted and joined
> —Kathy Fagan, "To a Reader"

If I could go back to Florence but could return to only two places, I know what they'd be: Vivoli Gelateria, on Via Isola Stinche in Santa Croce, and, just a short walk to the north, the Cloister of San Marco on Piazza San Marco. Gelato—that intense frozen mixture of whole milk, eggs, sugar, and whatever's ripe—soft and fast-melting like the silks still woven across the Arno at Antico Seitificio Fiorentino, which slide to the floor when you carry them.

this do in remembrance of me

In my own catechism, gelato means *all want, all desire, all appetite— the desire to be filled yet never full*—the names of the flavors themselves a litany that will almost suffice: *arancia, ciliegia, uva, pompelmo, mandarino, mirtillo, pesca, limone, pistacchio, panna, albicocca, crema, fragoline, albicocca, panna.*

to desire greatly; wish for

Even in the frescoes of Fra Angelico at San Marco, the hues of gelato appear, especially in the cells of the novices' dormitory, small rooms designed specifically for contemplation: the blood orange and peach robes of Gabriel and Mary in the *Annunciation* of Cell 3; on the wall of Cell 1, the creamsicle duet of Mary and Christ in the *Noli Me Tangere*; the pistachio canvas of the world in Cell 7, where *The Mocking of Christ* takes place, Christ enthroned at the center on his persimmon-colored box. In the *Presentation in the Temple*, Simeon arrives in a mint and lemon gown, the Christ Child swathed in whipped cream in his arms. Our *Tarocchio, pesca, panna e arancia, pistacchio, diaspora, menta, limone, panna.* At Christ's *Transfiguration*, the world turns out to be apricot, with an egg of whipped cream balanced at its center, and in the center of that egg is Christ, the letter *T. Albicocca, panna, T.*

to be without; lack

Yet despite their colors, the frescoes at San Marco—in accordance with their function as objects of spiritual contemplation—are *all absence of want and desire.* They enact, rather, the rituals—the *tableaux vivants*—of Christ's life and loss. There is perhaps no depiction of desire and imminent loss more moving than the one embodied in the figures of Mary and the *contrapposto* Christ in Giotto's *Noli Me Tangere* in the Scrovegni Chapel in Padua. In contrast to the palpable longing and tension of this fresco, however, Fra Angelico's *Noli Me Tangere* at San Marco conveys all the drama of an eighteenth-century minuet.

The Lord is my shepherd; I shall not want.

✦ ✦ ✦

But is it a good thing *to want, to have need for, to desire greatly,* even—to use the word as a noun—to have *pressing need,* to live in *want?* It's an intriguing word, one of those words in the language—like *cleave*—that can mean two opposite things. On the one hand, *to want* means *to lack, to be without*—to have some kind of emptiness. The word, however, also means *to desire greatly* to fill that emptiness—as in *filled with desire,* or *want.* Buddha tells us, of course, that to no longer want is preferable to wanting:

All life is suffering. All suffering is caused by desire. (The first and second noble truths)

Dante suggests, however, that whether we're on earth or in hell, *to want* may be our fate:

In this alone we suffer: cut off from hope, we live on in desire. (*The Inferno,* Canto IV)

✦ ✦ ✦

Albicocca, panna, the letter *T*; apricot and cream, the colors of Tom-Bon, our cat who died suddenly in October.

A PSALM OF STEIN

—Gertrude Stein, *Patriarchal Poetry*

> To be we to be to be we to be to be to be we to be we to be to be
> to be to be to be to be to be we we to be to be to be we to be.

> Let her be let her be let her be let her be to be to be let her be
> let her try.

> Let her let her let her let her try.
> Let her try.
> Let her try.
> Let her try.
> Let her be.
> Let her be let her
> Let her try.
> Let her be let her.[1]

> *Let her be / long. Let it be quick. Let her /*
> *be here. Let her not be / gone. Let her stay. Let her / go.*

❖ ❖ ❖

to request the presence of

Sometimes I'd like to think that in those last hours after the white tip of Tom-Bon's tail no longer responded to my voice, sometimes I'd like to think that it's a good thing she no longer knew *want*.

> *He maketh me to lie down in green pastures:*
> *he leadeth me beside the still waters.*

But what are the images of *not wanting?* The deer by the side of the road in positions we never imagined they could take, like the contortionists encountered in those black-and-white photographs found in old books about the circus: chin on the ground, knees akimbo above their head, a large bow of bone. The soft rag of her body no longer moving: the damp fur pushed back like waves that won't break, eyes open, mouth slightly ajar, staring ahead.

❖ ❖ ❖

Psalm 23 posits an end to, even a cure for, *want*, but how does that cure come about?

PSALM 23

1   The Lord is my shepherd; I shall not want.
2   He maketh me to lie down in green pastures: he leadeth me
    beside the still waters.
3   He restoreth my soul: he leadeth me in the paths of righteousness
    for his name's sake.
4   Yea, though I walk through the valley of the shadow of death, I will
    fear no evil: for thou art with me; thy rod and thy staff they comfort
    me.
5   Thou preparest a table before me in the presence of mine enemies:
    thou anointest my head with oil; my cup runneth over.
6   Surely goodness and mercy shall follow me all the days of my life:
    and I will dwell in the house of the Lord for ever.

Here is what the *Oxford Bible Commentary* has to say about the lines above:

> The happy confidence of this psalm, coupled with the comfort that it
> has given to those in "the valley of the shadow of death," have made it
> the best known and best loved of all the psalms. Later use has taken
> over from the original meaning, which is clouded in uncertainty. . . .
>   In fact the original meaning and setting of the psalm are completely
> unknown, and we are left with hypotheses and the more certain later
> use by Jews and Christians. . . .
>   The psalm is thought to have been used either in cultic ritual or in
> an act of worship reflecting the king's confidence.[2]

In Sunday school at the First Baptist Church of Wheaton, Maryland, we recited that psalm in the same uninflected, incantatory tone with which we chanted the Pledge of Allegiance each morning in public school: rising from our seats, we stared ahead, hand over heart, as if we were crossing patrols forever frozen into the signal for *come*. At the end of our recitation we sat down, and the day moved abruptly on. For those acquainted with Christianity, Psalm 23 is not only the most familiar psalm but also the simplest and most self-evident, the one least in need of explanation. It seems to provide comfort not only without revealing why but also without inciting questions as to how and why such comfort might arise.

> *He restoreth my soul: he leadeth me in the paths of righteousness*
> *for his name's sake.*

It *wants* explanation.

✦ ✦ ✦

to need or require

Even Saint Augustine in his multivolume *Expositions of the Psalms* devotes the briefest exposition—fewer than twenty sentences, in translation—to Psalm 23 (Psalm 22 in Augustine's Catholic version). As he explains it, the solace experienced here by the psalmist is simple and mysterious and, like all simple mysteries, miraculous:

> since my shepherd is the Lord Jesus Christ, I shall not lack anything. *In a place of fresh, green pasture he has set me*, for he has led me to faith in a field of fresh grass, and placed me there to feed me. . . .
> *And how excellent is your intoxicating chalice*, how excellent the chalice you give us to drink, which blots out the memory of earlier empty delights![3]

Central to Saint Augustine's interpretation of the psalms is, in fact, the miraculous: a kind of transubstantiation of the word on the page, whereby to recite a psalm is to experience the emotion of that psalm. Discussing this "'wonderful exchange' (*admirabile commercium*)," Michael Fiedrowicz in his introduction to Augustine's *Expositions of the Psalms* comments:

> It was precisely Augustine's conviction that the biblical words were inspired that enabled him to discover the necessary correction of such affections in the movement, typical of many psalms, from lament to trust and thanksgiving. If the emotional language of the psalms gives expression to rightly oriented affections—if indeed the psalm itself includes an *affectus*—this same emotion should be

aroused in the hearers. . . . As a consequence of the painful striving for affective adjustment to the psalms the inspired words may effect a transformation of one who prays.[4]

Dictum factum: said and done.

◆ ◆ ◆

to request the presence of

Yea, though I walk through the valley of the shadow of death, I will fear no evil: for thou art with me; thy rod and thy staff they comfort me.

Many of the Baptist hymns I learned as a child celebrate this comfort, this absence of want, made manifest through the presence—and words—of Christ. The hymn "In the Garden," in fact, is in many ways an enactment of Psalm 23:

> I come to the garden alone,
> While the dew is still on the roses,
> And the voice I hear, Falling on my ear,
> The Son of God discloses.

> And He walks with me, and He talks with me,
> And He tells me I am his own;
> And the joy we share as we tarry there,
> None other has ever known.[5]

But isn't this hymn in which a secret meeting in a garden is anticipated or recalled—this song that both celebrates and, in being sung, reenacts and creates intimacy, belonging, transcendence, and joy—isn't this hymn a love song? (Musically, too, it's a waltz; I used to alter the words, keeping the three-quarter-time rhythm, and sing, "And He walks with me and he waltzes with me.") And doesn't love imply desire or longing, *want*?

to feel an inclination toward; like

Edna St. Vincent Millay's elegy "Dirge without Music" is also a love song, but the final stanzas belie the possibility of curing us of *want*:

The answers quick and keen, the honest look, the laughter, the love,—
They are gone. They are gone to feed the roses. Elegant and curled
Is the blossom. Fragrant is the blossom. I know. But I do not approve.
More precious was the light in your eyes than all the roses in the world.

Down, down, down into the darkness of the grave
Gently they go, the beautiful, the tender, the kind;
Quietly they go, the intelligent, the witty, the brave.
I know. But I do not approve. And I am not resigned.[6]

◆ ◆ ◆

my cup runneth over

If I could go back, if I could have only two moments again with
Tom-Bon, what would they be? Tom on my lap, asleep finally; finally
not anxious, without want. But at the end, the thing I remember most,
although in all other ways she seemed unconscious, is the white tip of
her tail rising when I spoke.

Christopher Smart wrote what could be called "A Psalm of Cats."

For I will consider my Cat Jeoffry.
For he is the servant of the Living God, duly and daily serving him.
For at the first glance of the glory of God in the East he worships
    in his way.
For this is done by wreathing his body seven times round with elegant
    quickness.

· ·

For having done duty and received blessing he begins to consider himself.
For this he performs in ten degrees.
For first he looks upon his fore-paws to see if they are clean.
For secondly he kicks up behind to clear away there.
For thirdly he works it upon stretch with the fore-paws extended.
For fourthly he sharpens his paws by wood.
For fifthly he washes himself.
For sixthly he rolls upon wash.

· ·

For he purrs in thankfulness, when God tells him he's a good Cat.
For he is an instrument for the children to learn benevolence upon.
For every house is incompleat without him & a blessing is lacking in
    the spirit.

. . . .
For he knows that God is his Saviour.
For there is nothing sweeter than his peace when at rest.
For there is nothing brisker than his life when in motion.[7]

♦ ♦ ♦

Surely goodness and mercy shall follow me all the days of my life: and I will dwell in the house of the Lord for ever.

One recurring theme of the Psalms is what theologians term theodicy: the attempt to justify God's ways, given the existence of evil and suffering in the world. And one of the enduring mysteries of the Psalms remains that of how those who are experiencing pain or grief arrive at comfort, belief, and hope.

In his analysis of Psalm 73, for instance, James L. Crenshaw examines how the psalmist moves from the anguished doubt of a believer whose faith has been tested to a reaffirmation of his faith and trust in God. This shift occurs, according to Crenshaw, at a "turning point" in the psalm; trying to understand "the prosperity of the wicked" while he himself is "plagued, and chastened," the psalmist exclaims, "When I thought to know this, it *was* too painful for me; / Until I went into the sanctuary of God; *then* understood I their end" (73:3, 14, 16–17). Simply by entering the sanctuary, then, the psalmist is able to come to terms with the seeming good fortune of his enemies. Crenshaw explains it this way:

> Now at last the burden of trying to understand vanishes. . . . This new setting opens previously closed windows and allows fresh air to flow freely. The psalmist, as it were, takes a deep breath and shouts the discovery. . . .
>
> Having entered the sanctuary, the psalmist has become a new creature. The ignorance has disappeared, and so has the brutish stance before God. Now the picture is a domestic scene of a child and parent walking hand in hand. Divine presence is envisioned not as sporadic but as continual. The ancient promise "I shall be with you always" has become a reality in the psalmist's life.[8]

Crenshaw concludes, "The psalmist has stood near the flame and has at last been caught up in it."

A similar mysterious transformation underlies the certitude and faith of the believer in Psalm 23. If we read the psalms in sequence, Psalm 23 of course follows Psalm 22, one of the most anguished laments in the Bible (after Job's) and one that prefigures Christ's agony on the cross. Psalm 22 begins "My God, my God, why hast thou forsaken me? why art thou so far from helping me, and from the words of my roaring?" (22:1). The lament then continues until verse 22, when the psalmist abruptly shifts from pleas for salvation and deliverance to confident assertion: "I will declare thy name unto my brethren: in the midst of the congregation will I praise thee." The declaration builds for another nine verses until the psalm's climax, when the psalmist concludes, "They shall come, and shall declare his righteousness unto a people that shall be born, that he hath done this" (22:31).

I will declare . . .

What follows the end of Psalm 22 is a visual, spatial, and spiritual leap to Psalm 23, the kind of transcendent leap described by the poet Walt Whitman, paraphrasing the Bible, in *Song of Myself*: "Swiftly arose and spread around me the peace and knowledge that pass all the argument of the earth, / And I know that the hand of God is the promise of my own."[9] For Whitman, this moment arises out of the encounter—the lovemaking, even, if we follow his metaphor—between physical and spiritual, body and soul, individual human and limitless cosmos, and, certainly, between lovers. Most important for Whitman, however, in his song—or psalm—of himself, this moment of spiritual transcendence, assurance, and joy can also occur for the reader of his poem, rising out of the encounter between the reader and the words on the page.

◆ ◆ ◆

to seek with intent to capture

The Psalms are, at their most basic level, an attempt to praise God, and this attempt must of course be preceded by the desire or need to praise God—one must *want* to do it. The paradox of Psalm 23 is that it offers to fulfill desire by extinguishing *want* itself. Or perhaps the psalm simply embodies the paradox of the word *want*.

> but she makes hungry
> Where she most satisfies.[10]

The paradox of writing an essay on Psalm 23—"The Lord *is* my shepherd; I shall not want"—is that to *essai*, as Montaigne showed us, is to try, which is preceded by want, the desire to try. Out of more than a hundred essays, Montaigne never wrote an essay titled "Of want," most likely because that's the unwritten subtitle of all of his essays, all his attempts. "During the period of his conversion Augustine had seen his own existence interpreted by the psalms; but conversely his own story became an exposition of the biblical words."[11]

◆   ◆   ◆

to seek with intent to capture

Charles Baudelaire wrote that the only way to inhabit the present is to revisit it in a work of art. We might paraphrase Baudelaire and add that sometimes the present moment is so painful that the only way we can bear to inhabit it is to visit it in a work of art—in the case of Psalm 23, in a poem, a song, a spoken act/art. As a statement that both bears witness to the unbearable want and need that gives rise to it and, at the moment of utterance, redeems that need, Psalm 23 is what linguists term a "speech act"—to say it is to do it, as in "I promise" or "I pledge."

As Saint Augustine knew, Psalm 23 embodies nothing less than the sacrament of language, whereby the act of saying—enunciation—makes it so, brings it into being, and in this way reenacts the eternal mystery of the annunciation, whereby the word in the womb became flesh. Renunciation, enunciation, annunciation: it's the mystery of language itself. *Dictum factum*: said and done. For just that moment of speaking, whatever you say is there, briefer even than the taste of gelato or the light on the frescoes at San Marco.

At the end, a minute became a minuet, and Tom-Bon's last breath was the color of fresh-cut grass.

NOTES

1. Gertrude Stein, from "Patriarchal Poetry," in *Bee Time Vine: And Other Pieces, 1913–1927* (New Haven, CT: Yale University Press, 1953).

2. John Barton and John Muddiman, eds., *The Oxford Bible Commentary* (Oxford: Oxford University Press, 2001), 374.

3. Saint Augustine, *Expositions of the Psalms,* vol. 1, trans. Maria Boulding, ed. John E. Rotelle (New York: New City Press, 2000), 244–45.

4. Michael Fiedrowicz, Introduction to Rotelle, *Expositions of the Psalms,* 1:13–66; quote is from 1:41.

5. *Songs of Faith* (Nashville, TN: Southern Baptist Convention, 1933).

6. Edna St. Vincent Millay, "Dirge without Music," in *Collected Poems,* ed. Norma Millay (New York: Harper & Row, 1956).

7. Christopher Smart, "Jubilate Agno," in *The Collected Poems of Christopher Smart,* ed. Norman Callan (Cambridge, MA: Harvard University Press, 1967).

8. James L. Crenshaw, *The Psalms: An Introduction* (Grand Rapids, MI: William B. Eerdmans, 2001), 123, 126.

9. Walt Whitman, "Song of Myself," from *Leaves of Grass,* ed. Sculley Bradley and Harold W. Blodgett (New York: Norton, 1973), lines 91–92.

10. William Shakespeare, *Antony and Cleopatra,* in *William Shakespeare: The Complete Works,* ed. Alfred Harbage (Baltimore: Penguin, 1969).

11. Fiedrowicz, Introduction to *Expositions of the Psalms,* 1:39.

'TIS THE SEASON
Holidays, Harvests, and the Psalms

Lynn Domina

A week before Christmas, I sat in a decidedly low-rent pizza joint—our mall is too small to support a food court—mulling over my slice of primavera and eavesdropping on the group in the next booth. Two men, a bunch of kids, they spoke to each other with the slightly formal tone of acquaintances unaccustomed to the intimacy of a shared meal, even as casual a one as this. Then one girl in the next booth piped up: "We live at the very end of a dead-end road way up on the mountain, and we still decorate our house! We have a huge blue star that we put out in the yard and white snowflakes that we hang from the roof of our porch." Clearly proud of her family's enthusiasm, the girl spoke triumphantly, as if she had outwitted hordes of cynics who would have pointed to her empty road and asked, Why decorate if there's no one to ooh and ahh?

But of course holiday decorations most often fall within the expressive—rather than expository or persuasive—mode (a slogan like "Let's put Christ back in Christmas" proving the rule through its exceptionality). An expressive speaker sings and shouts whether or not anyone hears. The girl celebrated because the quality of celebration dwelt within her.

Driving home that evening, I did see a lone blue star—hers or a kindred spirit's—about a mile up the mountain, warding off the darkness on nearly the longest night of the year. I felt oddly but pleasurably lonely considering that star and the hands that had placed it there, turning it toward one of this rural county's few trafficked roads. Against the black sky, the blue lights shone distinctly, almost personal in their solitude, and I watched for it specifically on subsequent days through Epiphany, when even the most enthusiastic among us store away our decorations for another year.

A few minutes later, I entered the village limits and saw ahead a blaze of white light, almost appalling in its exuberance ("he must have $500 worth of lights out there")—lighted wire trees, lighted wire reindeer positioned sturdily on the lawn, icicle lights hanging from the eaves, blinking lights swirled around the porch posts, the entire north wall of the house aglow in an evergreen silhouette. Some people, I suspect, might not find this display entirely tasteful, as if emotion ever were tasteful. Taste is built, after all, on restraint, but creation is not. Creation assumes abundance.

In my own home, our Christmas decorating is immersed in good intention. This year, we did actually cut down a pine tree from our own yard, a truly exotic experience for two folks whose understanding of Christmas trees otherwise meant marching purposefully down Broadway to 116th or so and forking over fifty bucks to a guy from Jersey. When you cut down the smallest tree in your yard and drag it into your living room, however, you make certain discoveries about scale. So we trimmed off a few more branches, twirled it around several times, and realized that whichever side faced the wall, this pine was decidedly pear-shaped. Such is the choice of nature—moderate symmetry. But ornaments we had—an abundance of Santas—red, green, silver Santas, Santas hoisting evergreens, Santas puffing pipes; and birds—cardinals, chickadees, woodpeckers, one partridge perched beside a pear; and bears that should be sleeping through this northern December, and horses on a carousel, and little lambs and lions, and an English hedgehog, and one blue fish. I could go on—my memory unwrapping each ornament, crumpling the tissue paper, my memory delighting in itself— part of the memory of unwrapping each ornament the annual memory of its purchase in New York or New Hampshire or Michigan. Then I remember the moments before Christmases past, a decorated tree, its delicate lights, snowflakes illuminated by a streetlamp, the carols I listen to as I choose goofy wrapping paper for goofy gifts, beautiful paper for beautiful gifts, as I sip eggnog and hum along, *in excelsius De-e-o*. These moments fade into Christmas present.

In itself, Christmas doesn't generally lead me to the psalms—I'm more likely to recall the Magnificat, or the angels' admonition to the shepherds, "Be not afraid," or Isaiah as interpreted by Handel, "He shall be called wonderful"—but exuberance recalls the psalms, as does the romance of a white Christmas. Several years ago, I became friends with a Brazilian woman who was on an extended visit to the United States. Our first significant snow that year fell in mid-December. We clomped through the drifts as evening fell, then lay on our backs to make snow angels which did look like angels (who could have been afraid of anything that night?), my friend clapping her mittened hands under the coated trees and shouting, in her own new English, "I feel just like a children." Later, inside, our jackets steaming on the radiator, she gazed out the window. "Now, I know," she said. "Ice and snow, bless the Lord. Now I know what that means."

Now that I live in the country, in the mountains, I know too— "whence shall come my help." I recall that line from Psalm 121 almost daily, as I do lift up mine eyes to the mountains. I can hardly help it, gazing out my study window, ambling down the hill from my office. And each day is different—wisps of green in late spring, darkening through summer, tinges of blue at dusk or during light rain, rolling depth on clear days, indistinct edges through fog. Every day, they are the same mountains, calling my eyes to rest upon them, and yet they are never the same, eliciting an ineffable response that demands to be named— faith or hope that all things can be made new. All things can be made new, and a fundamental characteristic of human spirituality is, I think, a drive to renew the earth and ourselves, insistent as we nevertheless are on denying that desire.

The end of Psalm 121 I remember almost as often, climbing into our Subaru or settling into a 747, "God bless my coming and my going." The last phrase of the psalm, "now and forever," I recite by rote, though if truth be absolutely told, I don't trust "forever." Guard my coming and my going this time, just one more time, is what I actually mean. I won't hold you to forever. The psalm assures us that God "neither slumbers nor sleeps," but I fret nevertheless, buckling my seat belt—what if today is the day God nods off, just when life is getting good? My faith won't move mountains. Most days, gazing upon them is enough.

Like a few other sections of the Bible, the psalms hold forth some lines that are almost as significant out of context as they are in context—surprised as I am to hear myself say that, since one of my other fundamental beliefs is that verses out of context are the root of all evil. But whether we live in the city or the country, in the desert or at a river's edge, some lines from the psalms continue to speak to our daily lives, one reason perhaps why so many believers savor the psalms outside of formal liturgies. "God bless your comings and your goings." "A clean heart create for me, O God, and a steadfast spirit renew within me" (51:12). "Had I but wings like a dove, I would fly away and be at rest" (55:7). "You have prepared the land: drenching its furrows, breaking up its clods, softening it with showers" (65:11). "Now that I am old and gray, O God, forsake me not" (71:18).

Most days, I am most drawn to the psalms of praise, though less for their mood than their detail. Who was it who noticed that philosophers praise light, while poets praise the sun and moon? For what good is light if we can't follow the sun in its quest east to west? What good is light if we can't invent stories to explain the patterns of stars, the hunter with his bow, the bears who climbed to the sky? I turn to Psalm 148, which calls for praise in this way instead: "Praise God, sun and moon; praise God, all you shining stars." I read lines like this as statements of fact rather than commands, not that the sun and moon and shining stars *should* praise God, but that they do, in their blinking and blazing, through their beams and rays.

The psalms of praise suggest creation stories to me, especially the one narrated in the first chapter of Genesis. They list the elements of creation, all of the beings God called good. Psalm 148 continues:

Praise God from the earth,
     you sea monsters and all depths;
Fire and hail, snow and mist,
     storm winds that fulfill his word;

You mountains and all you hills,
    you fruit trees and all you cedars;
You wild beasts and all tame animals,
    you creeping things and you winged fowl. (148:7–10)

Everything that is, because it is, praises its creator. And there is so much, even among the great sea monsters, creatures that for modern folks like us often bump up against fantasy: killer whales and hammerhead sharks, the blue-ringed octopus floating among Pacific coral, the common octopus with its nearly human eye, the giant Pacific octopus expelling a cloud of ink, the short dark vampire squid, the longer lighter pacific squid, the awful giant squid whose corpse occasionally floats ashore. I imagine that even the monsters who don't exist praise God, the hydra and dragon, the basilisk and cockatrice.

Even the weather praises God—"hail, snow and mist, storm winds," the delicate rain outside my window now. When God encouraged the earth to bring forth vegetation—grasses and trees and moss and flowering plants—God prepared an equal range of precipitation, not just rain and snow, but drizzle and monsoon, sleet and deluge, shower and sprinkle and downpour. (Here is where I wish Eskimos really did use twenty different names for snow.) April showers, summer showers, pelting autumn sleet, praise God.

Wouldn't it have been sufficient, or at least more efficient, to create a one-size-fits-all style of precipitation? One weather pattern, one geographic feature, one species of vegetation? Wouldn't it have been sufficient to create one variety of apple, one of pear and orange? Well, no, because the creative spirit is boundless. So we have quince apple and crabapple, Macintosh and Golden Delicious, Granny Smith and Cortland. In our own garden, my partner, Sandra, and I have raised zucchini and pattipan squash, spaghetti squash (miniature and regular), butternut and delicata. Praise God you squashes and you beans, you tomato and you cucumber. Praise God you grubs and you slugs, even, you leaf-eating beetles, you foraging deer and rabbit.

Several years ago, someone instructed me that when my spirituality matured, it would become Christocentric. Even now, the memory irritates. Spirituality emerges from temperament. For me, and I suspect for many writers and other artists, even for those of us enthusiastically identifying with a Trinitarian tradition, the most compelling divine characteristic is not incarnation but creation. Out of nothing, we make something, or if not nothing, out of our imaginations, out of interminable gazing through windows, out of wonder and obsession. Or if not that, out of aphasia we grow articulate.

So I read all of the psalms, but when I skip to the good parts, it's to the details of creation. Psalm 104 is, in my New American edition, titled "Praise of God the Creator," specifically singling out this element of God's identity. Its organization follows, more or less, the sequence of creation in Genesis, citing the residents of "the heavens," the clouds and winds, first and then the features of earth, mountains and "the springs that wind among the mountains" (104:10). The psalmist proceeds to summarize the work of God, who gives drink to "every beast of the field," to birds and cattle and humanity. God produces "bread from the earth / and wine to gladden men's hearts, / so that their faces gleam with oil, / and bread fortifies the hearts of men" (104:14–15). God provides us the means, in other words, to celebrate our identity as God's creatures. Creation is itself every feast day's originary moment.

These psalms of praise often attempt to justify their inclination— God has saved or exalted or acknowledged the psalmist's community, and so the people give praise. Sometimes, however, the overt justification comprises a minor section of the psalm, as in 148. God "has lifted up the horn of his people," the psalmist asserts in the last verse. Until then, we readers might not have realized the psalm was about power. Rereading, we see that some of the references are to powerful creations—angels, sea monsters, fire—but others are not—tame animals, mist, fruit trees.

In Psalm 147, the writer enumerates the reasons why the people should praise God, but then it's as if the act of praise gets away from him. God has given you peace, the psalmist reminds us, and "blessed your children within you." As war often leads to famine, peace brings "the best of wheat," which the psalmist imagines ripens by virtue of God's language: "He sends forth his command to the earth; swiftly runs his word!" This personification of the word informs the psalmist's impulse to praise other acts:

> He spreads snow like wool;
>   frost he strews like ashes.
> He scatters his hail like crumbs;
>   before his cold the waters freeze.
> He sends his word and melts them;
>   he lets his breeze blow and the waters run. (147:16–18)

Again with the weather. Living in the country means attending to the weather. Three years ago, we bought a two-hundred-year-old house and quickly became acquainted with the local plumber. Hot water heaters, pressure tanks, cutoff valves, pumps—who knew? That first winter in the house, we had a spell of (really) cold weather. One night, when the temperature dropped to −25 degrees (I'm talking real temperature, not wind chill), a pipe leading upstairs froze and broke. Before God's cold, the waters froze; before God's powerful cold, water burst copper. We kept the pipe with its inch-long split, for we were filled with awe. "Look at this," we'd say to our city friends when they dared visit. And I learned to keep an eye on the thermometer; if the temperature reached zero before I went to bed, I set the faucets to drip. Some nights, I'd watch the temperature stagger downward from 7.5 as I brushed my teeth to 4.3 as I set my alarm, to 2.1 as I slid my pajama top over my head. I think that was the year Sandra started, after the model of our New Hampshire friends, sleeping in a stocking cap.

Of course, winters aren't always so cold. The temperature can remain comparatively mild—say, 25 degrees above zero—and drifts of snow will still accumulate to the garage roof. Actually this is a good thing, for if there's no snow on the ground in March, April arrives with drought warnings, just as one begins fantasizing about this year's garden. Of course, one doesn't actually put any plants in the ground until after Memorial Day. (Last year, I planted on Memorial Day, and Wednesday night my tomatoes suffered frostbite.) Planting peas on Good Friday is a tradition we've reluctantly abandoned with no ill effects. This year, the weather's been fine, plenty of rain, the promise of sun. And the cute little bunny that was hanging out near the apple tree and raspberry patch hopped right on over to the broccoli and lettuce. What a feast. I learned all about fencing. St. Paul says those who do not work shall not eat. I'm doing all the work here. Although I haven't yet sighted its twitchy little nose down the barrel of a shotgun, I've begun to understand the temptation.

Implicit in these psalms—121, 147, 148—and in many others is a sense of place, and of a person's relation to place. Out my window now I see tiger lilies praising God, and a blue spruce, and wild strawberries and mint. After a week in Florida, my memory sees palm trees and geckos, new images renewing my spirit. I suppose given time enough, I could have been at home there, among the Spanish moss and orange groves and humidity, but I just visited, my round-trip ticket purchased months ahead of time. We're home, or we're in exile, weeping on the shores of Babylon. We enter the marketplace and gaze on the myriad faces of those like us, or those who are not. We're home, or we're alien. Or we're home and we're alien, strangers in a strange land even as we pull into our own driveways. Many of us feel alienated at one time or another, I suspect; those of us targeted by hate groups or hate speech seldom completely settle in to the idea of home. As an out lesbian, I'm almost always at least somewhat alien. I read the letters to the editor; I know how enraged some people are that the breath of God fills my lungs too. So I plunge my hands into the earth, planting beans and cucumbers and gladiolus and renewing my spirit.

Until recently, I treated the geographical place in which I found myself as coincidence, as nearly irrelevant. Place was interesting if it was the place I'd go next, and even then I thought not so much about where I was but about what I'd do there. Nothing made me more impatient than people who talked about blooming where you're planted, as if a coconut palm could bloom in the Catskills if only it would. Doesn't the Bible also say something about going to the ends of the earth?

But now I'm undeniably approaching middle age and verging on settled. Occasionally, my stomach still revolts at the thought of staying put, so I hedge my bets; I'm here for the foreseeable future. Even so, I've learned to appreciate some of the advantages of a settled life. Knowing I'll be around for the harvest, I can plant a full garden. We're cultivating perennials in the flower beds. Although I probably didn't choose the best spot, I planted an asparagus bed last year. By next summer, we should be able to eat a few stalks. The future holds, perhaps, a strawberry patch, a raised koi pond. The trouble is, even amid my own restlessness, I love my own yard, its spaciousness, its promise, even the work it demands.

Of course, I've chosen this pastoral life in the region with the worst soil I've ever dug my hands into. The few grams of dirt that occasionally appear among the stones and rocks consist almost exclusively of clay. To compensate, we built raised beds, but even the topsoil we paid good money to have delivered was nothing but clay. Fortunately, our little acre is flanked by deciduous trees, so we till in a few bushels of leaves every spring, along with about sixty-five compressed feet of peat moss and a few bags of composted manure. One of the easiest ways to startle your city friends, we've discovered, is to drive around for a week with your backseat full of big white plastic bags stamped "cow manure."

By July, when the tomato plants' stems are thick and sturdy and the cucumber and squash vines climb the fence and entangle themselves across the lawn, the compost is ready. I spread spadefuls at the base of each plant, imagining the nutrients dissolving toward roots. Even more than creation, I think, decomposition and re-creation are miraculous. Imagine—a pile of dried leaves, a few banana peels, apple cores, peach pits, a bowl of coffee grounds, some turns with a pitchfork, hungry earthworms—and voilà, rich black new soil. I've seen it with my own eyes, sifted it with my own hands. "Praise God, you fruit trees and all you cedars," you leafy vegetables and root crops, you legumes and herbs. Yes, praise God you inedible husks and stems, for you shall renew the face of the earth.

Writing this essay, I've come to a new understanding of the connection between praise and renewal. The blue spruce in the middle of our backyard praises God with each spring's new growth, even as it drops its cones later in the season, even as so few of its seeds germinate. The rest go to prepare the soil for whichever one will come after. The rotting trunk of another fallen tree, feast to blissful termites, collapses into splinters and dust, spreads itself through the copse of living trees. With time enough, oxygen converts each of us into praise. Meanwhile, we renew ourselves and the earth, the ones who celebrate winter holidays with a blaze of light, the ones who gaze through windows preparing to write, the ones who turn the compost and fret about the seedlings.

UPON THE FLOODS

Diane Glancy

> I thought on my ways, and turned my feet
> to your testimonies.
> —Psalm 119:59

Last fall I drove 4,799 miles in a week and a half. From St. Paul to Portland, from Portland to Tulsa, from Tulsa back to St. Paul. I had to give readings in Portland, Oregon, and Vancouver, Washington. I had to be in Tulsa for the Nimrod Literary Journal's Pablo Neruda Poetry Prize. The trip also would be research for a book on Sacajawea. I needed to drive along the Columbia River and visit Fort Clatsop near Astoria, Oregon, where Lewis and Clark wintered in 1806.

I left St. Paul on a Tuesday afternoon after class because I had to be in Portland Friday and I wasn't sure how long it would take. I would spend the fall break driving. I did so by choice. I need to make migrations whenever possible. There is something integral for me in the movement over land.

As I started west on I-94 toward North Dakota, the late October trees were red; the sky, mauve; the underclouds, a brownish rust red. I listened to the Psalms as I drove. I wanted strength for the unknown journey ahead.

> To him who laid out the earth above the waters, for his mercy endures
> forever.
> To him who made great lights, for his mercy endures forever.
> The sun to rule by day, for his mercy endures forever.
> The moon and stars to rule by night, for his mercy endures forever.
> To him who struck Egypt in their firstborn, for his mercy endures forever.
> And brought Israel out from among them, for his mercy endures forever.
> To him who divided the Red Sea in two, for his mercy endures forever.
> And made Israel pass through the middle of it, for his mercy endures
> forever.
> But overthrew Pharaoh and his army in the Red Sea, for his mercy
> endures forever.

To him who led his people through the wilderness, for his mercy endures
forever.
To him who slew kings, for his mercy endures forever.
And gave their land for a heritage, for his mercy endures forever.
A heritage to Israel his servant, for his mercy endures forever.
Who remembered us in our low state, for his mercy endures forever.
And redeemed us from our enemies, for his mercy endures forever. (From
Psalm 136)

What I listened for in Psalms was mostly the landscape. "The outgo-
ings of the morning and evening, the rain, hills, rivers and valleys, the
settled furrows, the pastures of the wilderness clothed with flocks and
crops" (from Psalm 65).

In Psalm 24:1–2: The earth is the Lord's, and the fulness thereof; the
world, and they that dwell therein. For he founded it upon the seas, and
established it upon the floods.

In Psalm 74:17: He has set all the borders of the earth: he has made
summer and winter.

In Psalm 89:12: He created the north and the south.

In Psalm 121:2: My help comes from the Lord who made heaven and
earth.

In Psalm 46:1–2: God is my refuge. I will not fear though the earth
be removed.

The earth was removed as I drove. It was dark and I wanted to stay in
Bismarck, North Dakota, the first night. I kept driving. The headlights
of cars passed. The taillights of other cars passed. Some of the taillights
I passed.

I was alone under the sky. I was alone on the road though mountains
shook with rumbling; though the earth tumbled into dark, I kept driv-
ing. My refuge is in the Lord.

✦ ✦ ✦

The next day, Wednesday, I drove from Bismarck to Missoula, Montana.
I felt the momentum over the road as I drove. In Billings, I changed
from I-94 to I-90. I stopped at a drive-through, and ate a hamburger as
I drove. I wanted to keep moving.

The voice of the Lord shakes the wilderness. The Lord sits upon the flood. The voice of the Lord breaks the cedars. He makes them skip like calves. The voice of the Lord divides the flames of fire (from Psalm 29).

Before I left St. Paul, I had watched the leaves on campus fall in flames. I had raked the red leaves below the maple in my yard. Along the road, I knew the sumac were the first to turn. Jesus, Lord of the flames.

+ + +

The next day, I left Missoula before dawn.

Psalm 119:148: "My eyes are awake through the night watches, that I may meditate on your word." I heard night watches as nightwatchers. I thought of the deer and night animals; their red eyes like embers.

Psalm 144: "Bow down your heavens, O Lord, come down; touch the mountains until they smoke." I knew I was in the mountains as I drove the winding road through the dark. Lord Christ, the stars are witness to the dark.

It was dawn by the time I drove across the narrow strait of northern Idaho. I got breakfast in another drive-through in Spokane, Washington. At midday I was on 395 driving south in eastern Washington toward I-84 in Oregon.

In Psalm 147:8: You cover the heavens with clouds.

When the highway along the Columbia River turned white with lightning, and the sky seemed a moon without a sky, Jesus is Lord.

+ + +

Thursday evening, I was in Portland at the Mountain Writer's House. I went to bed early. In the stillness of a nearly twelve-hour dead sleep, Jesus is.

> You cover yourself with light:
> you stretch out the heavens as a curtain:
> you lay the beams of your rooms in the waters:

you make the clouds your chariot:
you walk on the wings of the wind.
You lay the foundations of the earth.
You cover it with the deep as with a garment: the waters stood above the
mountains.
At your rebuke they fled; at the voice of your thunder, they went away.
They go up to the mountains, they go down by the valleys to the places
you founded for them.
You set a bound they may not pass over; that they turn not again to cover
the earth.
You send the springs into the valleys, which run among the hills.
They give drink to the animals of the field.
By them the fowls of the heaven have their habitation, which sing among
the branches.
You water the hills from your chambers.
You cause the grass to grow for the cattle.
The trees of the Lord are full of sap; where birds make their nests: as for
the stork, the fir trees are her house.
The hills are a refuge for the wild goats; and the rocks for badgers.
You appoint the moon for seasons; the sun knows his going down.
You make darkness, and it is night: when the animals creep.
The lions roar after their prey, and seek their meat from God.
The sun rises, they gather themselves together, and lay down in their dens.
Man goes to his work and labors until the evening.
Lord, how manifold are your works! in wisdom you have made them all.
So is this great and wide sea, wherein are things creeping innumerable.
There go the ships, there is that leviathan, whom you made to play therein.
You look on the earth and it trembles; you touch the hills, and they smoke.
(From Psalm 104)

From Friday to the following Tuesday, I read at Pacific, Clackamas,
and Clark Colleges. On Saturday, I drove to Fort Clatsop along the
Pacific Coast and took notes for my manuscript on Sacajawea.

At Fort Clatsop I picked up a rock. Whenever I'm writing, I take
something from the land. It's where I get the voices I want to write.

Psalm 18:2: The Lord is my rock.

Psalm 18:31: Who is a rock save our God?

Psalm 18:46: Blessed be the rock.

Psalm 27:5: In the time of trouble he sets me on a rock.

Psalm 28:1: Unto you I cry, O Lord my rock.

Psalm 31:3: You are my rock.

Psalm 40:2: You set my feet upon a rock.

Psalm 42:9: I say to God my rock, why have you forgotten me?

Psalm 61:2: I cry to you when my heart is overwhelmed: lead me to the rock that is higher than I.

Psalm 78:16: He smote the rock, and the waters gushed out.

Psalm 92:15: He is my rock.

Psalm 95:1: The rock is my salvation.

Near Astoria, I climbed a hill and looked out to the ocean.

In Psalm 95:5, The sea is his and he made it: and his hands formed the dry land.

In Psalm 98:7–8, Let the sea roar, and the fulness thereof; and they that dwell therein. Let the floods clap their hands.

Lewis and Clark knew uncertainty every step of their voyage. The weather, the lack of provisions, the numerous Indian tribes that outnumbered them along both rivers and on the coast. Last summer I had driven the Missouri River as I began research on the book.

Psalm 107:22–30: They that go down to the sea in ships, and do business in great waters, These are the works of the Lord, and his wonders in the deep. For he commands and raises the stormy winds, which lifts up the waves. They mount up to heavens; they go down again to the depths; their soul is melted because of trouble. They reel to and fro, and stagger like a drunken man, and are at their wit's end. Then they cry to the Lord in their trouble, and he brings them out of their distresses. He makes the storm a calm, so that the waves are still. Then they are glad because they are quiet; so he brings them to their desired haven.

All of Psalms seems to be a divided highway. Cries of agonies and desperate pleas for help mixed with continuous, profound praise of the Lord's faithfulness.

In several verses in Psalms, the earth is built upon the floods or rivers or seas. In other words, the earth and our lives upon it are built upon uncertainty and contradiction.

Many native creation myths and explanation tales are about a piece of mud placed on the waters that eventually spreads out into dry land that animals can inhabit. Every tribe has a story of dry ground coming to the water, of meaning coming from chaos.

✦ ✦ ✦

Jesus make it alright.
—Sonny and Brownie, CD 0829

On Tuesday, after a noon reading at Clark College in Vancouver, Washington, I started to Oklahoma. The first night I stayed in southeastern Oregon. The next day, on my way through Utah on I-84 toward I-80, on an overpass, the rear tire blew. There was a moment I didn't know which way the car would go. But the car stayed on the road as it slowed and I pulled to the side once I was across the overpass. A man behind me stopped and changed the tire. He said he had seen it happen. He thought the car would flip.

Afterward, I drove through the Wasatch mountains east of Provo on I-84 toward Wyoming.

I cried by myself in the car from the release of tension. The near catastrophe. The loneliness of the road. My only companion, the living God who made the universe.

Psalm 84:3: The sparrow has found a home, and the swallow a nest.

Psalm 102:6–7: I am a pelican of the wilderness; I am an owl of the desert. I am a sparrow alone on the house top.

That night I stayed in southeastern Wyoming. The next night in northern Oklahoma just under the Kansas border. Besides the Psalms, I also listened to the journals of Lewis and Clark on tape as I traveled east through Colorado and Kansas, thinking of the expedition, thinking a voice, Sacajawea's, into being. Listening to King David of the Old Testament. Thinking of his endurance the afternoons I was weary of driving. Looking for a place to stop for food. No one to talk to about the experience of travel.

Early Friday afternoon, I was in Tulsa.

Saturday night, after the Nimrod ceremonies, I started back to St. Paul. I stayed in Kansas City the first night, then drove to St. Paul the next day.

◆ ◆ ◆

During the journey, I also listened to the Psalms for weather. In my thirteen years in Minnesota, I have felt snow, ice, blizzard, extreme cold, and the uncertainty of weather. But there isn't much snow in Psalms. I have to go to Job for winter. Job knew the cold.

Job 37:6: By the breath of God frost is given.

Job 38:22: Have you entered the storehouses of snow? Have you seen the hail?

But I was in Psalms on this trip, and it was not yet winter, though snow can fall in October, especially late October. I remembered that before the trip I thought, *If I can just get through North Dakota and Montana.*

I think it snows only four times in Psalms, and the first two snows are abstract.

Psalm 51:7: Wash me and I am whiter than snow.

Psalm 68:14: When the Almighty scattered kings, it was *white* like snow in Zalmon.

But finally, Psalm 147:16–18: He gives snow like wool; he scatters the hoarfrost like ashes. He casts his ice like morsels; who can stand before his cold? [But then] He sends out his word and melts them; he causes his winds to blow.

Job 37:6: He said to the snow, be on earth.

Psalm 148:8: Fire and hail; snow and vapor, stormy wind fulfilling his word.

◆ ◆ ◆

Psalm 19:1: The heavens declare the glory of God; and the firmament shows his handiwork.

I know the difference between creation and creator. The creator is the object of praise. The creation is the result of the creator's work. Creation is one of the ways in which God is known.

From Psalm 114: When Israel went out of Egypt, the house of Jacob from a people of strange language, the sea saw it and fled. The Jordan was driven back. The mountains skipped like rams, the little hills like lambs. What's the matter, sea, that you fled, and Jordan, that you were driven back? You mountains, that you skipped like rams, you little hills, like lambs. Tremble at the presence of the Lord, at the presence of the God of Jacob, who turned the rock into water, the flint into a fountain.

It is the creator who is the object of praise; creation is one of God's subjects. Scriptures say that the creation is one of the ways God makes himself known.

From Psalm 148: Praise the Lord, earth and sea, mountains and hills, trees and cedars, beasts and cattle, creeping things and fowl.

◆ ◆ ◆

It seemed, in the end, that the landscape David wrote about was a landscape of faith. A migration across the circumstances he met.

I could enter the Psalms as I traveled. I could drive the road like a trucker. I could praise God before his creation. It seemed to me this is a day in which common man has access to God, and so does common woman. Faith has broken down the partition. I can enter a close relationship to God like David. I can do so because of Christ.

◆ ◆ ◆

I am reading Lyn Hejinian's *The Language of Inquiry*:

> Poetry comes to know things that are. But this is not knowledge in the strictest sense; it is, rather, acknowledgment—and that constitutes a sort of unknowning. To know *that* things are is not to know *what* they are, and to know *that* without *what* is to know otherness (i.e., the unknown and perhaps unknowable). Poetry undertakes acknowledgment as a preservation of otherness—a notion that can be offered in a political, as well as epistemological, context.

For poetry I could substitute faith. A thought process by which the unknown can be known, not really known, but gotten to as closely as possible. An unleafing of red from the trees. The politics and epistemology of Psalms: God is.

Sometimes I listened to different tapes as I drove, not always paying attention to order, but letting the psalms roll past as a moving landscape, taking the psalms out of context, out of chronological order, out of their numbered world, knowing that each psalm had a place within the Psalms, and each verse had its place within the psalm, I disordered the order, distangling and tangling it again on a knotted twine so that one tape was strung to another in a different, postmodern, biblical way, the testimonies of which were the road show; the passing landscape as it stood out from other travels; the summations of Psalms in the hallowedness of driving across the country at great expense, the motels at night, the gasoline, the flood of imagery, the climbing of the mountain in eastern Oregon on the way into Idaho.

Be with me, Lord, as I look into the fierce holiness of your word.

In Isaiah 6, the seraphim could hold a coal in his hand, but he had to lift it from the altar with tongs. No one can touch your holiness, O God, but something that has touched your altar can touch us.

On the road, I looked for these messages, these visions. I-94 from St. Paul to Billings, Montana. I-90 across western Montana and northern Idaho to 395 in Washington. 395 to 82 south to I-84 in Oregon to Portland.

Afterward, I-84 to Ogden, Utah. I-80 across Wyoming to I-25 south in Colorado to I-70 in Denver. I-70 across Kansas to I-35 south. The Cimarron Turnpike to Tulsa.

Then, I-44 to I-71 north to I-35 in Kansas City to St. Paul.

The road would stay with me. It would pass when I sat at my desk. When I walked to school.

On the trip, I had driven through the empty waters of the old sea, the prairie basin of dry land, joining biblical landscape and the passing terrain.

"THE DEVICES AND DESIRES OF OUR OWN HEARTS"

Reflections on Blessing and Curse in the Songs of Ascent

Robert A. Ayres

After the lullabies of my infancy, and the nursery rhymes of my pre-school days, the Psalms were the poems in which I was most thoroughly immersed. A cradle Episcopalian, born to a churchgoing family, I also spent seventeen of the twenty-one years of my formal schooling, including two years in seminary, attending Episcopal schools where worship was an integral part of the daily round. Not only are the Psalms read or sung as a distinct element of nearly every service, but threads of the Psalter are woven throughout the fabric of Anglican liturgy.

I remember the morning Mrs. Finkbeiner announced that each student in her sixth-grade class at St. Luke's would memorize a psalm. After flipping through the Psalter in the back of the family prayer book, I decided I would memorize both verses of Psalm 117, prompting Mrs. Finkbeiner to amend her assignment to stipulate some minimum number of verses. I settled on Psalm 121 (eight verses) and set about the task of memorizing it.

I suspect that had I been asked, I would have been hard pressed to give a reason for my selection. What I do know is that Mrs. Finkbeiner must have made this assignment early in the fall of that school year, sometime before the sixth of November 1969, the day my great-grandfather Ayres died. I was born on his eighty-fifth birthday. His given name, Atlee, is my middle name. He lived in San Antonio, where I grew up. We visited him Sundays after church, since he lived, with my great-grandmother Katherine, in a house on Belknap, just down the street from Christ Church.

Both the church and the house were products of his architectural imagination, but it was from the living room of his home that he was buried. What I remember of the service—the first funeral I ever attended—is that we read in unison Psalm 121, the one I had memorized for Mrs. Finkbeiner. *I know this*, I must have said to myself. I had become a vested participant in the service. I knew the words. I knew them by heart.

To speak this psalm out loud, by memory, on this occasion, placed me in a particular relationship to both text and tradition. On that November day, an eleven-year-old boy stood among a group of worshippers at a funeral in San Antonio, Texas, reciting a version of a psalm which, though continually revised to incorporate the findings of modern biblical studies, nonetheless retains the rhythmic textures and the linguistic flavor of Coverdale's 1535 English translation from the old Latin Psalter, which was itself a translation of the Greek Septuagint, translated from the Hebrew in Alexandria beginning in the third century B.C.E. And the underlying Hebrew psalm, written perhaps in the sixth century BCE, displays linguistic and stylistic elements borrowed from Canaanite poetry that scholars now recognize as the precursor of ancient Hebrew poetry.

Here is the version I memorized, from the 1928 Book of Common Prayer:

PSALM 121. *LEVAVI OCULOS.*

1   I will lift up mine eyes unto the hills; * from whence cometh my help?
2   My help cometh even from the LORD, * who hath made heaven and earth.
3   He will not suffer thy foot to be moved; * and he that keepeth thee will not sleep.
4   Behold, he that keepeth Israel * shall neither slumber nor sleep.
5   The LORD himself is thy keeper; * the LORD is thy defence upon thy right hand;
6   So that the sun shall not burn thee by day, * neither the moon by night.
7   The LORD shall preserve thee from all evil; * yea, it is even he that shall keep thy soul.
8   The LORD shall preserve thy going out, and thy coming in, * from this time forth for evermore.

I suspect I was drawn to the repeated words and phrases, and undoubtedly they helped me memorize the poem. These repetitions are even more pronounced in the Hebrew text than in most English translations, which typically substitute synonyms for at least some of the repeated words. Actually, the repeated words are often cognates or conjugations of a repeated verbal root, making the repetitions more nuanced and interesting in the Hebrew and at the same time more difficult to translate to English without resorting to synonyms. The following translation by the scholar Mitchell Dahood uses variations of the word "guard" to indicate all occurrences of words derived from the Hebrew verb שׁמר, for which the prayer-book translation uses both "keep" and "preserve." Dahood also adheres more closely to the literal word order of the Hebrew, allowing us to see the stairstep structure of the poem, where a word appearing in the second part of one verse is repeated in the first part of the following verse. This literary device may have served as a mnemonic aid. (I have indicated all variations of שׁמר in bold, and other words that occur in repetitive constructs in italics.)

PSALM 121

1 *A song of ascents.*

   I raise my eyes to the Mountain,
   whence will *help* come to me?
2 My *help* comes from the home of YHWH,
   who made heaven and earth.
3 He shall not put your foot in the Quagmire,
   your **guardian** shall not *slumber*.
4 Indeed he never *slumbers* nor sleeps,
   the **guardian** of Israel.
5 YHWH is your **guardian**,
   YHWH is your shade,
   the Most High is your right hand.
6 By day the sun
   will not strike you
   Nor the moon at night.
7 YHWH will **guard** you
   from every evil

He will **guard** your life.
8 YHWH will **guard** your going and your coming,
from now unto eternity.[1]

This psalm would have been recited responsively in a liturgical set-ting.[2] Verses 1–2 consist of a rhetorical question and answer, spoken in the first person by the worshipper—a declaration of faith in YHWH as the source of help and security—and concluding with the formulaic expression "who made heaven and earth." (Note that the repeated "help," in stairstep construction, occurs in both the question and the answer.)

Verses 3–8 constitute the response, the pronouncement of blessing, spoken in the second person, presumably by a priest or cultic official, and concluding with another formulaic expression: "from now unto eternity."

Perhaps it was this language of blessing that attracted me to Psalm 121 in the first place. Blessings were familiar to me. Liturgical blessings were said by the priest at the conclusion of Sunday services and the daily chapel services at St. Luke's. And there were special blessings for children—birthday blessings and the like. But there were also rituals of blessing even closer to home. We said blessings at mealtimes. And somewhere along the way, my mother and I had developed our own reciprocal blessing. After the requisite "God bless so-and-so's," and once I was tucked in for the night, she would say: "Jesus bless him and keep him safely through the night." I would answer, "Jesus bless her and keep her safely through the night."

On the cusp of adolescence (our bedtime ritual must have ended already by then, or would soon), and on the occasion of the death of my great-grandfather, for whom I had been named, might I have been look-ing to the larger community (and through that community to God), for help, for solid footing, and for blessing?

It wasn't long before notions of blessing were tinged with adolescent longings. As a teen, I became immersed in the lay renewal movement within the Episcopal Church, and the charismatic movement flourish-ing throughout the country in the mid-1970s. I remember traveling to Jacksonville, Florida, to attend a Faith Alive Weekend. Throughout the weekend, participants would share their witness—stories of how God's presence was transforming their lives—and we sang hymns from the hymnals of our more evangelical Protestant kin. For the teens the climax of the weekend was a late-night gathering in the candlelit sanctuary. We sat cross-legged around the altar on the wine-red carpet, surrounded by dark paneling and the smell of smoke and melting wax. We sang softly, a cappella or accompanied by guitar, holding hands and hugging one another, giving our lives to Jesus, ecstatic, our bodies tingling with desire.

Over the course of the weekend, I bonded with a girl named Candy, a girl with fair skin and straight white hair. We swapped addresses and promised to write, and we did, futilely plotting impossible reunions, until our affections drifted inevitably to others closer at hand. In one of my letters I asked her for a picture, which she sent me, along with a passage of scripture she had copied from Numbers. It was the Aaronic blessing scholars now believe lies behind the language of blessing in the Psalms,[3] and I memorized it:

> The LORD bless you and keep you;
> the LORD make his face to shine upon you, and be gracious unto you;
> the LORD lift up his countenance upon you and give you peace.
> (Numbers 6: 24–26, NRSV)

To these memories, I add another nocturne. A few years later, as an undergraduate at the University of the South in Sewanee, Tennessee, I often returned from the library to my dorm via the cathedralesque chapel to join a handful of students around the organ for Compline. Compline, from the Latin *complere*, to complete, "originated in the fourth century as the night prayers of monks in their dormitories."[4] We waited in silence, or whispered softly in the cavernous dark, listening to the breathy sounds of the organ warming up, until the bell in Breslin Tower had rung its ten solemn chimes. The student officiant sang the opening sentences, and we responded in a sung dialogue comprised of phrases and sentences borrowed largely from the Psalms. "The Lord Almighty grant us a peaceful night and a perfect end. *Amen.*" The next lines are from Psalm 121:2:

Officiant: Our help is in the name of the Lord;
People: The maker of heaven and earth.

A psalm is read—several are given to choose from—including Psalm 134, associated with Compline since at least the time of Benedict in the sixth century.[5] This short psalm is the last of the Songs of Ascent.

1　Behold now, bless the LORD, all you servants of the LORD,
　　you that stand by night in the house of the LORD.
2　Lift up your hands in the holy place and bless the LORD;
　　the LORD who made heaven and earth bless you out of Zion.
　　(Book of Common Prayer, 1979)

The congregation exhorts the priests to bless YHWH (verse 1 and 2a); the priest(s) reply with the blessing in verse 2b. "The two are a kind of mirror image of each other. God's action of blessing the worshipper is reciprocal to the human action of blessing God."[6]

The divine name YHWH appears in each part of each line. And there is the threefold repetition of "blessing," and the threefold reference to the place of blessing: "the house of the LORD" / "the holy place" / "Zion." Like a musical piece which ends with the chord of the key in which the piece is written, the second part of the second verse contains all three: the blessing, its source (YHWH), and its place (the temple in Jerusalem).

Toward the end of Compline, the officiant says a collect for those in need of special care or protection through the night hours. God is exhorted to "keep watch," "bless the dying," and "shield the joyous": "Keep watch, dear Lord, with those who work, or watch, or weep this night, and give your angels charge over those who sleep. Tend the sick, Lord Christ; give rest to the weary; bless the dying, soothe the suffering, pity the afflicted, shield the joyous; and all for your love's sake. *Amen.*"[7]

The service concludes with blessings, which in form mirror the opening sentences:

Officiant: Let us bless the Lord.
People: Thanks be to God.

The almighty and merciful Lord, Father, Son, and Holy Spirit, bless us
　　and keep us. *Amen.*

Standing together in All Saints Chapel, the colors of the towering stained glass windows muted in the low light, living for the first time far away from home, we gathered to say our bedtime prayers and blessings.

It so happens that the university's motto, *Ecce quam bonum*, "How good it is," is the beginning of Psalm 133, the penultimate psalm in the Songs of Ascent.

1　Oh, how good and pleasant it is, *
　　when brethren live together in unity!
2　It is like fine oil upon the head *
　　that runs down upon the beard,
3　Upon the beard of Aaron, *
　　and runs down upon the collar of his robe.
4　It is like the dew of Hermon *
　　that falls upon the hills of Zion.
5　For there the Lord has ordained the blessing: *
　　life for evermore. (Book of Common of Prayer, 1979)

Given the ideal of creating a community of learning rooted in Episcopal liturgical tradition, it is not surprising that the university selected this motto. The ornate vestments and vessels (I remember especially one giant, jewel-studded chalice), the sophisticated choral settings (some dating back to the Middle Ages) sung by the university choir, the Casavant Frères organ, the liberal use of incense, the gothic grandeur of the space itself, the superabundance of clergy and bishops—in sum, an adulation of all things ancient and Anglican—meant that the anointing of Aaron the high priest might have occurred in All Saints Chapel on any given Sunday without so much as the raising of an eyebrow.

Although the movement of the Songs of Ascent is generally upward—much lifting up of eyes and hands and voices to the hills and to the heavens—all reinforced formally by stairstep parallelism, in this psalm the same device is employed to express a movement downward. Having made the pilgrimage up to Jerusalem, having climbed the Temple steps, having raised their eyes and their hands in prayer and supplication, the faithful have extended themselves physically and spiritually as far as they can. The blessing they long for comes down upon them from above, liberally, like the anointing oil, and like the dew.

This copious dew, falling on Mt. Hermon, would also have held meaning for the university's founders. Sewanee, located atop the Cumberland Plateau in southeastern Tennessee, and affectionately referred to by the initiated as "The Mountain," is famous for its thick and drippy fog. The stained glass window above the altar depicts Christ the King enthroned and, at his feet, All Saints Chapel perched atop "The Mountain"! On either side of "The Mountain" is the procession of saints, martyrs, bishops—the faithful throng ascending toward the chapel in a deliberate linking of blessing and place.

Walter Brueggemann, in his book *The Message of the Prophets*, divides the Psalms into two broad categories: psalms of orientation and psalms of disorientation. Psalm 133 is a classic example of a psalm of orientation. In these poems, life "is not troubled or threatened, but is seen as the well-ordered world intended by God. . . . Life is experienced as protected space. Chaos is not present to us and is not permitted a hearing in this well-ordered world. . . . Such a satisfied and assured assertion of orderliness probably comes from the well-off, from the economically secure and the politically significant. That is, such religious conviction comes from those who experience life as good, generous, and reliable."[8] If Brueggemann accurately describes the psalms we have examined thus far, he fairly describes my life experience, at least through my college years, and life in the Episcopal Church as I knew it.

My next formal engagement with the Psalms occurred in the context of my graduate work at Virginia Theological Seminary in the early 1980s. Part of the learning was experiential, part academic. The 1979 revision of the Book of Common Prayer incorporated the discoveries and insights of a widespread liturgical renewal that had been fermenting within the church for years. Numerous changes were made in the Episcopal liturgy. Many were actually the incorporation of rediscovered rites and practices of the early church. The Psalms were now recited responsively by half verse, emphasizing the poetic quality of the psalms, and the workings of parallelism in particular. Previously, in my experience, the psalms had been read in unison, or responsively by the whole verse. Now, simply to recite the psalms, day by day at Morning Prayer in the seminary chapel, was to gain new insight into the psalms as poetry.

In the classroom I learned the principles of critical biblical scholarship, in particular the various schools of criticism that, beginning in the eighteenth and nineteenth centuries, enabled scholars to consider biblical texts in the light of the sociohistoric, linguistic, and literary advances developing in other disciplines during this same period. Form, literary, redaction, and textual criticism led to rich reassessments of biblical interpretation. But many of the scholarly breakthroughs pertaining to the poetics of the psalms have occurred more recently still, within the last fifty to seventy-five years, as archeological discoveries of poetic texts from Israelite and neighboring cultures and languages (especially Ugaritic) enable scholars to trace the origin and development of ancient Hebrew poetry.

I also studied Hebrew, acquiring a rudimentary knowledge of the language that allowed me to read the psalms (with heavy reliance on a good lexicon) and to recite them in Hebrew, albeit in the rather peculiar pronunciation scheme favored by Christian Old Testament scholars.

I learned to recognize the various literary genres within the Psalms and to consider their *Sitz im Leben* or "life setting" for the people who first composed and recited them.

I also discovered that there are several independent poetic collections within the book of Psalms and that many of my favorite psalms belonged to one of these collections, fifteen consecutive psalms (120–34) that all contain a similar heading, variously translated as "Song of Ascents," "Song of Degrees," "Pilgrim Song," and so forth. Other elements reinforce the theory that these psalms were a distinct collection. Six phrases, or formulas, occur in more than one psalm in the group. For example, in Psalm 121, the phrase "who hath made heaven and earth" (121:2) also appears in Psalms 124 and 134; and the phrase "from this time forth for evermore" (121:8) appears in Psalms 125 and 131. As I had already discovered, looking for a psalm to memorize for Mrs. Finkbeiner, these psalms are shorter than most (with the exception of 132, which many scholars believe to be several centuries older than the group as a whole). Most of the poems in the collection are generally considered to have been written in the late seventh century and early sixth century B.C.E., after the return from the Babylonian exile and following the construction of the Second Temple.

In spite of the linguistic and literary similarity among these psalms, they are a highly diverse group so far as genre is concerned. There are personal and communal laments (120, 123, 126, 129), a penitential psalm (130), a song of thanksgiving (124), a royal psalm (132), psalms in the wisdom tradition (127–28, 133), a liturgical psalm (134), a song of Zion (122), and a song of trust (121).[9]

Numerous linguistic inconsistencies suggest that a single author could not have written the entire collection. In what sense, then, do these poems cohere as a collection? The most convincing explanation I have encountered to date is proposed by Loren D. Crow, who observed that the psalms in the middle of the collection share certain characteristics, linguistic and stylistic, linking them with North Israelite traditions. On the other hand, poems that frame the beginning and end of the collection (121–22, 133–34) show strong evidence of ties to Jerusalem and the Temple cult. Crow believes a redactor added these "bookend" poems to an even earlier collection. He believes that the repeated formulas, along with other verses that reinforce the redactor's theological and political agenda, were added to the existing poems. This redactor, Crow posits, sought to encourage Jews in outlying areas to pledge allegiance to Jerusalem as the geographic and spiritual center of Jewish life in the postexilic period. The placement of 120 at the beginning of the collection (see the discussion on 120 below), and the inclusion of 122, a pilgrimage song, create the narrative construct of a pilgrimage, leading Crow to propose that the collection would have been used devotionally by Jews living in outlying areas in making pilgrimage to Jerusalem, perhaps for the principal festivals of the Jewish year. That most of the poems show a Northern Israelite provenance reveals a strategy on the part of the redactor designed to appeal to a targeted audience.[10]

The main weakness in Crow's hypothesis, from my perspective, is that the poems he feels were added to the collection share many of the stylistic features of the core group, whereas the collection as a whole shares stylistic qualities that sets it apart from most of the other psalms. One could perhaps argue that the postexilic poets closely associated with Jerusalem, and those in the outlying provinces in the same time period, were all influenced by the same poetic trends.

Without any assurance of absolute certainty—welcome to the world of critical biblical scholarship—Crow's hypothesis at least gives us a way of thinking about the Songs of Ascent as a group of poems within a particular literary and historical context, collected and edited by someone with a particular theological and political agenda.

Fast forward, ten years or so, to the summer of 1995. Back in Sewanee for the summer, I attended a Centering Prayer workshop to learn a form of meditation based on monastic disciplines of contemplative prayer in Western Christianity. Along with the practice of silence, I learned the discipline of *lectio divina*, which I have come to think of as a meditative rumination on a particular passage of scripture that holds special meaning or that challenges the reader in some particular way. Most of the passages that we read in the workshop, and in the subsequent Centering Prayer groups that I have attended, are from the Psalms. As a result, I found myself more intimately engaged with the Psalms than ever before in my life.

I had recently completed my MFA in creative writing. I sensed that there was subject matter, personal and sociopolitical, that concerned me deeply but that had not yet found its way into the poetry I was writing—largely, quasi-confessional free verse narrative in the prevalent style of the writing workshop. Some of the unexpressed material was related to longing, and to a deep discontent, something approaching lament. In the Psalms, I knew, lay a whole sea of discontent, an ocean of lamentation. But how do the Psalms work, as poetic speech, as lyric poems? Even though I had learned to read poems with a writerly interest in craft, the poetics of the Psalms escaped me. I embarked on an exploration of biblical poetics, particularly the workings of parallelism, the complex relationship between the two (or more) distinct parts of a line or verse of Hebrew poetry. "Like rhyme, regular meter, and alliteration in other poetic systems, [parallelism] is a convention of linguistic 'coupling' that contributes to the special unity and to the memorability (literal and figurative) of the utterances, in the sense that they are an emphatic, balanced, and elevated kind of discourse, perhaps ultimately rooted in a magical conception of language as potent performance."[11]

I made the perplexing and frustrating realization that Psalm 121, and the other poems of the Songs of Ascent, adhere only loosely to the stylistic workings of classical Hebrew poetry I was learning about (including parallelism, a loosely patterned rhythmic texture, and stock word pairs that provided the recurring imagery of the Psalms). Yet these psalms strike me as accomplished works of poetry. This conundrum led me in turn to closer readings in the Songs of Ascent.

These poets are clearly skilled in the techniques of fully developed parallelism. Within these parallel constructions they employ anaphora (especially in syntactic constructions), aural and semantic punning, and consonance. The length of the lines and the patterns of rhythmic stress are typical as well. And they draw freely from the available reservoir of stock word pairs—day/night, sleep/slumber, Zion/Jerusalem, walls/towers. (I think of these word pairs as akin to the predictable rhymes of country-and-western music—love/dove, blue/shoe, heart/apart. Like Homer's ornamental epithets, stock word pairs may have been an especially valuable tool for poets in a time of oral composition and recitation.)

But these poets did not limit themselves to the stock word pairs. They exhibit a willingness to incorporate in their poems fresh, even striking, images, along with archaic stylistic devices such as stairstep parallelism.

Three short laments within the Songs of Ascent reveal the stylistic accomplishment of these poets. They also exemplify what Brueggemann calls "psalms of disorientation." They reveal the lament as a form well suited for grappling with the dark side of human experience. On the one hand, they lament the effects of speech turned to malevolent ends, and on the other, they themselves employ virulent forms of speech in the literary form of the curse.

PSALM 120

1 In my distress I called to the LORD
   and He answered me.
2 O LORD, save me from treacherous lips,
   from a deceitful tongue!
3 What can you profit,
   what can you gain,
   O deceitful tongue?
4 A warrior's sharp arrows,
   with hot coals of broom-wood.
5 Woe is me, that I live with Meshech,
   that I dwell among the clans of Kedar.
6 Too long have I dwelt with those who hate peace.
7 I am all peace;
   but when I speak,
   they are for war. (*Tanakh*, 1261)

An individual lament, this poem is a distress cry of someone who
has been the victim of slander or malicious betrayal and who cries out
to YHWH for deliverance.

The lament as a poetic form is three-dimensional, expressing concern
over the speaker's relationship to God, to others, and to self.[12] In Psalm
120, the lament addresses each in turn. Verse 2 is spoken to YHWH;
verses 3–4 address the "deceitful tongue" as the personification of the
ones who have wronged the psalmist by their hurtful talk; and in verses
5–7 the speaker addresses his own condition.

Though variations are common, Brueggemann describes the struc-
ture of the lament as follows (the verse numbers in parentheses show
the placement of these elements in Psalm 120):[13]

Invocation: "O LORD . . ." (verse 2)
Complaint: "Woe is me . . ." (verses 5–6)
Petition: "Save me from treacherous lips . . ." (verse 2)
Motivation: (a reason why God should care/act): In this case, God's
   saving action in the past gives the speaker the confidence to address
   God now. (verse 1, though this element more typically occurs toward the end
   of a lament)
Imprecation: "What can you profit . . ." (verses 3–4)

If the form and structure of the lament guide the faithful through the darkness, through moments of life out of kilter, it is the stylistic force of parallelism that creates the lyric intensity of the lament. Several elements of parallelism as a poetic device are evident in verse 5.

> Woe is me, that I live with Meshech,
>> that I dwell among the clans of Kedar.

The verb in the first part of the line, "live" (גור), is mirrored by an approximately synonymous verb, "dwell" (שכן), in the second part. Meshech, a region far to the north in Asia Minor, is set in parallel relation to Kedar, a Bedouin tribe associated with the Arabian peninsula to the south.[14] The terms are in contrast, so far as their location is concerned, but similar in their expression of distance or remoteness from Israel, and perhaps in their animosity toward the speaker.[15] The ellipsis of the verb in the second part allows space within the rhythmic constraints of the line for a slight elaboration—in the first part, only the name of the place, "Meshech," is given; in the second part, we have "the clans of Kedar."

Similarly, in verse 2:

> O LORD, save me from treacherous lips,
>> from a deceitful tongue!

In the second part of the line, "deceitful" is parallel to "treacherous," and "tongue" is parallel to "lips," and both are stock word pairs. The shorter second part reflects the smaller number of stressed syllables, just two, compared to three in the first part. Verses 1–2 of the poem reflect the 3/2 rhythmic pattern common to the lament, with its limping effect.

Repeated syntactic elements reflect one type of repetition common throughout the Psalms. The other, also evident in this psalm, is the literal repetition of key words and phrases, an archaic practice generally avoided in developed forms of parallelism.

There are two such repetitions in the first part of the poem, and two in the second part. In the first part, YHWH is repeated in the first and second verses. In the first verse, he is referred to in the third person;

in the second verse, he is addressed in the second person. The phrase "deceitful tongue" in the second part of the second verse is repeated again at the end of the third.

In the second part of the poem, the verb "dwell" appears in the second part of verse 5 and is repeated at the beginning of verse 6. "Peace," the last word of verse 6, is repeated at the beginning of verse 7.

Crow observes that repetition "is a more subtle poetic device than first appears. It is primarily through this 'step' device that the poet makes transitions between lines that at first blush have little to do with each other."[16]

In Psalm 120, the poet decries the destructive power of human speech, likening it to sharp arrows and, in parallel construction, to hot broomwood coals. Arrows typically appear in parallel construction with swords in the Psalms and elsewhere, or as a metaphor for lightning. This is one of only three references in Hebrew scripture to the broomwood plant, a desert shrub still valued by Bedouin tribes for the hot-burning charcoal made from its root,[17] and the only occurrence where it appears in a parallel construction with imagery of warfare or destruction. Vivid imagery, where we might otherwise expect to find stock word pairs, makes these psalms more accessible and interesting to modern readers.

In the opening psalm of the Songs of Ascent, we find a lone figure, far removed from the cultic center of his world, advocating peace, surrounded by people eager for war. In the redacted narrative construct of the Songs of Ascent, this is the first psalm in the collection, the pilgrim's starting point, a far cry from the exuberant *ecce quam bonum* of the gathered community (Psalm 133). This is the place, literally and figuratively, from which the pilgrim must "lift his eyes" to the hills, or to Jerusalem, or to the heavens, as in Psalm 123, another terse lament.

1 To you I lift up my eyes,*
   to you enthroned in the heavens.
2 As the eyes of servants look to the hand of their masters,*
   and the eyes of a maid to the hand of her mistress,
3 So our eyes look to the LORD our God,*
   until he show us mercy.

4 Have mercy upon us, O LORD, have mercy,
 for we have had more than enough of contempt,
5 Too much of the scorn of the indolent rich,*
 and of the derision of the proud. (Book of Common Prayer, 1979)

Like Psalm 120, this poem begins with an invocation in the first-person singular, but it shifts immediately to the first-person plural, suggesting that the lament was written for, or adapted to, communal use in a liturgical setting. Presumably the leader would say the opening line, and the worshippers would join in at the second verse.[18] The repetition of the word "eyes" links the two parts and may serve as well as a verbal prompt for the congregation. The continued repetition of "eyes"—four times in the first three lines—suggests a fierce attention, a fixation of the faithful on YHWH as the source of their deliverance. This fixation is reinforced by the striking image of servants with their eyes glued to the hand of their mistress or master—watching every move, waiting perhaps to be fed or to be shown some kindness.[19]

The corporate plea for mercy (verse 4) further underscores the presumed liturgical setting. The line occurs almost verbatim in the Book of Common Prayer in Suffrages B in the service for Morning Prayer, a pastiche composed entirely of lines from various psalms. The versicle (V) and response (R) are recited responsively between the officiant and the congregation.

V. Save your people, Lord, and bless your inheritance;
R. Govern and uphold them, now and always.
V. Day by day we bless you;
R. We praise your Name for ever.
V. Lord, keep us from all sin today;
R. Have mercy on us Lord, have mercy.
V. Lord, show us your mercy;
R. For we put our trust in you.
V. In you, Lord, is our hope;
R. And we shall never hope in vain.

As in the Songs of Ascent, the repetition of "mercy," "bless," and "hope" creates a stairstep effect within the suffrages.

The first and third verses of Psalm 123 are examples of a common type of parallelism in which the second part of the line is simply an extension or expansion of some aspect of the first part, in this case merely a comma, or pause between phrases within the line. Verse 4 is also an extension, only in this case the second part, "for we have had more than enough of contempt," provides the reason for which the supplicants are pleading for the Lord's mercy. Verses 2 and 5 show a combination of repeated and substituted elements. In verse 2, "eyes" and "hands" are repeated, while "maid" is substituted for "servants" and "mistress" is substituted for "masters." These morphologic pairs are another stylistic device characteristic of parallelism, and distinct from the stock word pairs we have already discussed. Words of the same class (noun, verb, etc.) may contrast in tense, conjugation, person, number, gender, or definiteness. These nuances are often lost in translation, but in this case they are transparent—nouns contrasting in both number and gender. While I selected the Book of Common Prayer translation for the literary qualities of last two verses, it does mask some of the repeated words, which are evident in Loren Crow's more literal translation:

> Have mercy on us, O YHWH, have mercy on us;
> For we have had our *fill* of **contempt**!
> Our souls are utterly *filled up*
> With the ridicule of those at ease,
> With the **contempt** of the haughty![20]

This community has tasted the humiliating sting of servitude—it still smarts in the collective memory.

> Whether this speech articulates, illuminates, or evokes experience, it does move the awareness and imagination of the speaker away from life well-ordered into an arena of terror, raggedness, and hurt. In some sense this speech is a visceral release of the realities and imagination that have been censored, denied, or held in check by the dominant claims of society. For that reason, it does not surprise us that these psalms tend to hyperbole, vivid imagery, and statements that offend "proper" and civil religious sensitivities. . . . They are speech "at the limit," speaking about experience "at the limit."[21]

The lament is not only the domain of the afflicted individual; like African American work songs and spirituals, the lament gives voice to the complaint of a people who have known oppression and degrading servitude.

PSALM 129

1 Since my youth they have often assailed me,
      let Israel now declare,
2 since my youth they have often assailed me,
      but they have never overcome me.
3 Plowmen plowed across my back;
      they made long furrows.
4 The LORD, the righteous one,
      has snapped the cords of the wicked.
5 Let all who hate Zion
      fall back in disgrace.
6 Let them be like grass on roofs
      that fades before it can be pulled up,
7 that affords no handful for the reaper,
      no armful for the gatherer of sheaves,
8 no exchange with passerby:
      "The blessing of the Lord be upon you."
      "We bless you by the name of the LORD." (*Tanakh*, 1265–66)

The leader recites the opening line, then prompts the congregation to join in the recitation. Together they repeat the first line and proceed. While the entire poem is in the first-person singular, the individual clearly stands for the nation (verses 1b, 5a).

As the *Tanakh* translation suggests, the poem is in two parts: In the first part, past oppression and deliverance at the hand of YHWH are remembered, and the second part may be regarded as a curse, though the enemies here are not addressed directly.[22] The verbs occur in the jussive tense, and it should be assumed that YHWH would effect the fulfillment of the curse.

With the exception of verse 5, which invokes imagery of warfare, the imagery is drawn from the world of subsistence agriculture.[23] In the graphic image of verse 3, Israel is plowed ground; her oppressor is the plowman. The repetition of "plow" (in nominal and verbal forms) in the same line suggests the back-and-forth action of plowing, and the furrows suggest the deep wounds left by the lashes of a whip. The imagery shifts slightly in verse 4—Israel here appears to be the beast of burden (which also would have been whipped), free now from the cords that held it to the plow.

The poem ends with a second agricultural image: a piddling harvest of withered grass, growing where it doesn't belong—an ingenious curse wherein the actions of the harvesters are actually predicated on what will not come to pass. The last line of the poem is the blessing a passerby would exchange with a harvest worker,[24] a blessing that is not to be.

The curse, like the blessing, is a literary genre in its own right, with roots in magic. In these formulations, the words themselves, by virtue of their content and the form of their expression, contained the power to bring about the thing spoken.[25]

Brueggemann suggests that within the dramatic structure of the lament the poet moves toward a moment of cathartic imprecation, "regressive . . . unguarded language that in most religious discourse is censored and precluded. . . . This is the voice of resentment and vengeance that will not be satisfied until God works retaliation on those who have done the wrong. . . . In these psalms of disorientation, as life collapses, the old disciplines and safeguards also collapse. One speaks unguardedly about how it in fact is."[26]

Small wonder I passed over these laments in my search for a psalm to memorize for Mrs. Finkbeiner, notwithstanding the obvious appeal of their brevity. As an eleven-year-old growing up in an affluent niche of America, insulated by and large from the chaos of the 1960s, I had no way to identify with the raw outbursts of individuals lamenting treacherous deception and betrayal, much less the lamentations of an ancient people speaking from the experience of brutal oppression. Certainly nothing in my religious upbringing would have led me to conceive of this language as an appropriate way to talk to God—or to anyone else, for that matter.

The vicissitudes of my own life experience have given me a new appreciation for the individual laments. And the ethnic, tribal, and sectarian bloodshed which we witness in an unprecedented way through the media make the communal laments, written 2,700 years ago, shockingly contemporaneous and resonant today.

These poems emerged from a poetic tradition elastic enough to embrace both blessing and curse, to celebrate life as it should be—and sometimes is—and to lament what is fractured and out of sorts in the life of the individual and in the world at large. Some of the finest examples of each type of psalm, when judged by the criteria of literary craft, occur in the Songs of Ascent. The liturgical form of these psalms reveals that this material made its way not only into preserved poetic speech but also into the language of liturgy—literally, "the work of the people." Had it not, we probably would not be reading them today. The Songs of Ascent were arranged by an editor who understood life "to be a pilgrimage or process through the darkness that belongs properly to humanness."[27] The end of this journey is a place, a sacred space, where there is blessing in the company of one's fellows, where, in the words of Psalm 126,

> Those who sowed with tears
>   will reap with songs of joy.
> Those who go out weeping, carrying the seed,
>   will come again with joy, shouldering their sheaves.

NOTES

1. Mitchell Dahood, *Psalms III*, vol. 17A of *The Anchor Bible* (New York: Doubleday, 1970), 199.

2. Hermann Gunkel, *An Introduction to the Psalms* (Macon, GA: Mercer University Press, 1998), 314.

3. J. Day, *Psalms* (Sheffield, UK: Sheffield Academic Press, 1992), 68.

4. Marion J. Hatchett, *Commentary on the American Prayer Book* (San Francisco: Harper, 1995), 144.

5. Ibid.

6. Loren D. Crow, *The Songs of Ascent (Psalms 120–134): Their Place in Israelite History and Religion* (Atlanta: Scholar's Press, 1996), 127.

7. 1979 Book of Common Prayer.

8. Walter Brueggemann, *The Message of the Psalms* (Minneapolis: Augsburg, 1984), 25–27.

9. Bernhard H. Anderson, *Out of the Depths: The Psalms Speak for Us Today*, 3d ed. (Louisville: Westminster John Knox, 2000), 223.

10. Crow, *The Songs of Ascent*, 186–87.

11. Robert Alter, *The Art of Biblical Poetry* (New York: Basic Books, 1985), 9.

12. Patrick D. Miller, *Interpreting the Psalms* (Philadelphia: Fortress, 1986), 48.

13. Brueggemann, *The Message of the Psalms*, 54–57.

14. Dahood, *Psalms III*, 197.

15. Crow, *The Songs of Ascent*, 34.

16. Ibid., 35.

17. Dahood, *Psalms III*, 197.

18. Crow, *The Songs of Ascent*, 49.

19. Dahood, *Psalms III*, 209.

20. Crow, *The Songs of Ascent*, 48.

21. Brueggemann, *The Message of the Psalms*, 53.

22. Dahood, *Psalms III*, 230.

23. Crow, *The Songs of Ascent*, 82–84.

24. Gunkel, *An Introduction to the Psalms*, 223; Dahood, *Psalms III*, 233.

25. Gunkel, *An Introduction to the Psalms*, 222–23.

26. Brueggemann, *The Message of the Psalms*, 55.

27. Ibid., 52.

REREADING THE PSALMS

Janet McCann

I first really listened to Psalms when I was in grade school and my
maternal grandfather was dying. This was my first family death. I had
been told very little about my grandfather's illness, except that he was
in the hospital. I was not allowed to visit him, but my mother drove
me past the hospital and I waved to him, or at least to a tiny figure way
up high on a balcony she said was my grandfather. I knew something
bad was happening, but no one would tell me anything, except that he
was supposed to come home soon and I should try to stop pestering
everybody. I sensed an extreme tension in the air, in everyone's voice;
my mother enrolled me in a local Bible school, where we received bird
stickers for learning Psalms. I was a fast learner and soon had a whole
aviary. The Psalms I learned then I still mostly have, unlike the poems
and mnemonics they taught me in school. Saying them over and over
to learn them engraved them on my brain and alleviated the heavy,
unnamed fear that seemed to hover over all of us.

My grandfather did not return home, and I never saw him again.
The funeral was probably a quiet closed-casket event, but in any case
children of my milieu were not taught anything much about death and
were kept from funerals—shunted off to a friend's house, or to Bible
school, for everything death-related. Afterward, they told me he had
cancer but was supposed to recover from the operation and be all right
for a few months. They didn't want to tell me he would die, they said, as
that would ruin my last months with him. This was in the beginning of
the 1950s, and I don't think they do death that way anymore; certainly,
when my mother died, I mishandled it differently with my children.
During my grandfather's illness I recited my newly learned Psalms over

and over, never with anyone near, as it seemed to me to be a secret practice no one should know about. I thought it would only cause my family alarm, as did most practices I picked up outside the home somehow.

We were not a Bible family. We went to the Presbyterian Church on Christmas and Easter and some other times too, when someone thought about it. Mostly we spent Sunday mornings in the tiny living room surrounded by newspapers, reading about Maggie and Jiggs, Denny Dimwit, Blondie and Dagwood. We were a middle-middle-class family who always struggled with bills but managed to own our own little frame house of the sort associated with the 1930s and 1940s. I think the year before my grandfather died we got our first car—it was a round-looking white Ford. We did not absolutely have to have a car, as my father took the train into the city every morning and walked the half-mile to the station. After we got the car, we were in the proud line of mamas and children waiting to pick Dad up at the station every afternoon at five-thirty. It was like picking the kids up from school.

But this essay is about the Psalms and how they functioned in my life. I always knew the Twenty-third Psalm, even before the illness of Grandpa, whom I called Duffy. Since my family did not read the Bible I don't know where I got it—school, perhaps, the "morning exercises" that included the Pledge of Allegiance, the Lord's Prayer, and a Bible reading. But the Psalm became more vivid when he was in the hospital. "Though I walk through the valley of the shadow of death, I will fear no evil, for Thou art with me." I had no idea what "thy rod and thy staff" were but they comforted me. Duffy entered the valley; I trusted God to take care of him. I said the psalm with my prayers at night, most of which were simple, repeated phrases, or short prayers I was taught—I thought it important to repeat each prayer five times, though not the psalm. That was always recited last, and I think it was for me a kind of quilt to cover myself with before sleep. I didn't like my assigned prayer, "If I should die before I wake / I pray the Lord my soul to take." I wanted to be followed by goodness and mercy and dwell in the house of the Lord forever.

Still, the Twenty-third Psalm has a sadness to it for me, together with the consolation: I see the valley of the shadow of death. Which is not in some of the newer versions, where it becomes simply "the valley of death"—disappointing, more like something out of Tolkien, compared to my beloved KJV, which to me as a child was The Bible. (I read the psalm again recently when my best friend from college was dying of cancer—she loved it, wanted it read again and again, together with the 121st Psalm. She was a Buddhist, but she drew her dying comfort from the Psalms. And she liked that line, too—felt as though death was hovering over her, and would get her, but she would not be alone: that to her was the promise of the psalm.)

After childhood I met the Psalms again formally as a freshman in college in 1960, when they were presented as part of a literature class. I was told that they represented phases of the Covenant—the Covenant established, broken, reestablished. The cycle didn't seem to work very well for me when I tried to apply them to the Psalms as I read them. The Psalms did not seem to be approachable as literature in any way—they did not unpack neatly like the poems of John Donne or T. S. Eliot. No background information or careful tracing of the lines yielded a meaning that was then mine, to put in my mental pocket like the understanding of Donne's compass image. Rather, they were treacherous, sometimes meaning something overwhelming but ineffable, sometimes something opaque and incommunicative. I resented the instructor telling me what they meant, when that was not what I felt they meant.

Now as an older adult—golden ager? Senior citizen? I reread the Psalms and they speak to me again, but differently. They are frightening and beautiful: frightening because of how warlike they are, how much they seem to be asking for God's military support. I feel very tiny, reading them, menaced on all sides by creatures out of my grandson's imagination: My Enemies. The landscape I see is bleak, flat, menacing—what comes to mind is the no-man's-land accursed in Isaiah, the place where, according to one translation only, Lilith can find rest among the barren branches and other wild creatures. The speaker who is the reader is in pain, beset. I/She is hungry, thirsty. I/She implores the God whom she has trusted to provide solace, support, another landscape. He does. The other landscape provided has hills, mountains, running water that is the living source. Valleys are green; olives, figs, and dates grow there.

The trouble for me is that these two landscapes flicker back and forth like one of those children's code rings I used to find in cereal boxes: now one scene, now the other, changing with the slant of the ring. Here are hills, figs, water, comfort; there is flatness, agony, the extreme of agitation, despair. Now one, now the other.

The flicker effect may be caused by the fact that the Psalms are personal in an intense way that is not characteristic of much of the Bible. The pleading, pain, rejoicing, and praise come from a voice that is immediate, merging with the reader's interior voice; the reader cannot get away from it. Whatever the speaker feels is a sharp image in the reader's mind, and the images replace each other as the tone changes. There are indeed cycles of pain and praise, but they are not any abstract or conceptual covenant, they are the phases of a single soul in its relationship with God. God is there, immediately; or the speaker is looking for him, but cannot find him; or the speaker is filled with gratitude for rescue; or the speaker doesn't understand why rescue has not come. The speaker's consciousness is much more present than the Enemy, whatever or whoever that may be. There are only three presences: the speaker, God, and the Enemy, who moves in the margin like a dragon on the edge of the map.

Sometimes the Enemy is supplanted by the Wicked, who are enemies of God as well as or instead of the speaker; the Wicked turn the psalm into a series of oppositions: this is how the righteous are, this is how the wicked are. But the speaker's voice, as he weighs and balances, seems to dominate—the poem is still about the speaker and God, the human mind trying to figure out the nature of things, trying to understand how divine justice functions on earth and how it applies to one particular sentience.

What emerges for me finally is the total isolation of the self, a minute particle of fire possessed with the desire to rejoin the flame. I don't see society, politics, community—anything much concerning the relationships between or among people. I see only this burning twig, this self, and its need for the completion of being absorbed in the other. The Enemy need not be human, and in fact in my vision of the Psalms it is not. There are the nightmare creatures, which can be inside as well as out—they are whatever prevents the union between the self and God. The flickering self prays for deliverance, doesn't understand why and how these enemies spring up, doesn't have the means of combating them. I tend to divorce the Psalms from all contexts and empty them of time and place—something I have been told not to do, but do anyway, automatically. I think many people who read the Psalms repeatedly do the same thing.

To write about them, I tried to learn more about them, but found that this process impeded rather than enhanced my experience of them. The Psalms simply are. It might or might not be interesting to read that the rod and the staff were "a club about 30 inches long, [often with] flint or bits of iron embedded in it" and "about 6 feet long . . . used in Israel to count the sheep."[1] I already knew they were the apparatus of the shepherd; they both kept the sheep in line and gave them a sense of the shepherd's concern for and awareness of them. As a child I pictured Jesus as the shepherd, with that omnipresent sweet Jesus image popular in the 1940s—and still, for that matter. He had a cane in one hand and in the other something like a shillelah, perhaps to keep errant sheep in line, though that did not go with the image.

The Psalms to me need no gloss, not even to know who wrote them, or when. There is just that voice, asking the questions we all ask: Where are you? Why do you not succor me? Why do my enemies prosper? If I am good, am I not to be rewarded? I have sinned; can I be forgiven? If I die, where will I be then? The shy attempt at influence: God, if you kill me, how can I praise you? You won't be able to hear my songs from the underworld. Deliver me, so I can continue to do you honor. These are the intimate questions, the I and thou of the soul and God. We find many voices in the Bible, but no other voice quite like this. (I read that the Psalms were written by a number of authors, but to me they are one voice, all those separate pleas and praises joined.) These are prayers of us each individually, modified by our pressing concerns of the moment. There is a nakedness about the voice, expressing a vulnerability and an openness that is needed for the communication to be complete, that is, for God to answer it. But we don't always hear the answers; sometimes we hear only the questions. They are often agonized questions, the ones that lie at the boundaries of faith and doubt, hope and fear.

Because for me the Psalms are so intensely personal, I prefer to read them alone, just as I did as a child. I want to let the voice drive out my own voices and speak in their place. I don't like to be interrupted, as this reading is a meditative experience, although when I am contemplating the Psalms I am not consciously meditating, which I do at other times. I seem to be speaking and reading the words at once, the voice both inside and out. It is work reading the Psalms, and I have little energy to spare for their loveliness as literature—unlike, for instance, when I read Ecclesiastes, which I think I experience as a fine essay. And for me the Song of Solomon is a lush poem. But the Psalms are work, the work of facing the hardest questions and waiting, listening intently for God's answer. Of course the Psalms are only one half of the dialogue, the words of the naked soul. God's answers must be inferred, and sometimes, in psalms of triumph and of consolation, they are clear. God has intervened, he has vanquished the enemy and restored the speaker. Joy and praise pour forth. It does not matter much to the reader exactly who the enemy was or how the speaker has triumphed—his exaltation is witness to God's rescue. The particular psalms with the strongest pull for me, though, are of two types—supplication and quiet gratitude.

In the supplicatory psalms I feel the voice asking questions, listening for response. An immense energy goes into the listening. They are sometimes dark-night-of-the-soul psalms, with a certain impatience to the questions: Why? Why is the balance of justice not visible? "How long wilt thou forget me, O LORD? for ever? how long wilt thou hide thy face from me? How long shall I take counsel in my soul, having sorrow in my heart daily? how long shall mine enemy be exalted over me?" (13:1–2.) Consolation may follow soon in the same psalm, or may not. "Hold up my goings in thy paths, that my footsteps slip not. I have called upon thee, for thou wilt hear me, O God: incline thine ear unto me, and hear my speech. Shew thy marvellous lovingkindness, O thou that savest by thy right hand them which put their trust in thee from those that rise up against them. Keep me as the apple of thine eye, hide me under the shadow of thy wings, From the wicked that oppress me, from my deadly enemies, who compass me about" (17:5–9). Even in the supplication the feeling of protection and comfort reigns: the thought of being the apple of God's eye, in the shadow of his wings, separates the speaker already from the menacing enemy. The speaker is special, chosen to bear God's favor, even if at the moment the results of this favor are not visible.

Quiet gratitude and musical praise characterize the poems that mark the fulfillment of God's promise. These are statements of faith that express a sense of God's presence, or else shouts of joy; I tend to prefer the quiet ones, although the joy of the noisy ones is contagious. The speaker compares love for God to things that may astound: I love you more than fat, more than meat. The physical world is fruitful and prosperous; the blight has been lifted. "Thou crownest the year with thy goodness; and thy paths drop fatness. They drop upon the pastures of the wilderness: and the little hills rejoice on every side. The pastures are clothed with flocks; the valleys also are covered over with corn; they shout for joy, they also sing" (65:11–13).

The Psalms can be used as aids to meditation by reading part of one or a whole short one and reflecting upon it, then going into the traditional meditation with the echoes of the psalm still in the mind. I find the image of fruition just quoted as especially conducive to peace of mind: God's answer, the pastures "clothed with" sheep, the valleys filled with corn, "covered over" with it. In the joyous psalms the sense of the desperate individual diminishes and there is a sense of community.

A friend and colleague, poet David Craig, has written Psalms poems that intrigue me partly because they emphasize what for me is paramount: the sense of the intense isolation of the human soul, the desire for God that grows in this isolation. Here is one sample:

PSALM #7

Yahweh, if I am to die,
let it be in the sweet scythe
of Your wood.

Rise, You who demand justice
bear Your name
Look past intention.
Look at this face, a cooling fire,
these hands, winter leaves.

God preserves what He has pierced.

Give thanks to Yahweh,
whose voice creaks in the starry wood,
the whole place alive somehow
with water. Heavy grasses, green,
dark with it, and I feel the
same night the foliage does,
recite the same verses.
My body, too, belongs to the great
material curve of this planet, sky.
It is who I am, this way and
terminus. It haunts my every
blind and faithful step with the
signature of what we are, the promise
of where we live.[2]

The part of the psalm that generated the meditation:

1 O LORD my God, in thee do I put my trust: save me from all them that
   persecute me, and deliver me:
2 Lest he tear my soul like a lion, rending it in pieces, while there is none
   to deliver.
3 O LORD my God, If I have done this; if there be iniquity in my hands;
4 If I have rewarded evil unto him that was at peace with me; (yea, I have
   delivered him that without cause is mine enemy:)
5 Let the enemy persecute my soul, and take it; yea, let him tread down
   my life upon the earth, and lay mine honour in the dust. Selah.
6 Arise, O LORD, in thine anger, lift up thyself because of the rage of
   mine enemies: and awake for me to the judgment that thou hast
   commanded.

7 So shall the congregation of the people compass thee about: for their sakes therefore return thou on high.

8 The LORD shall judge the people: judge me, O LORD, according to my righteousness, and according to mine integrity that is in me.

Poems about the Psalms have been written by many, and I am always encouraged to find a new approach to the Psalms—or even to find a line of one used as an epigraph. The language of the psalm invariably outshines the poem, but nevertheless the poems often provide spiritual satisfaction as the voice of the poet blends with the Bible speaker. I have tried to write my own Psalms poems, but find I cannot—they are too huge for me. I sit in awe before them, pen hovering over empty page. I have to accept the appreciation of others. It is a pity that there exists no anthology of individual poets' reactions to specific psalms, including the texts of the Psalms with the poems; in such a book the reader would be able to see how others have responded to the Psalms with their own songs, and experience the different kinds of vibrations poets have experienced from their reading, the Psalms becoming the palimpsest of spiritual struggle over the years.

My adult return to the Psalms has changed them and has not. I can now see the distress in some of them, the pleas and the listening. I am more willing now to engage with the more difficult passages, those that may indeed require some research and reading for comprehension, and also those that focus on the enemies and on the pain of trying to reach God rather than the joy of having done so, and the peace that follows. The Psalms remain a comforter, but they are no longer a quilt.

NOTES

1. Information about rod and staff is from G. Christian Weiss, *Insights into Bible Times and Customs* (Lincoln, NE: Back to the Bible Press, 1972).

2. David Craig's poem, included in his book *The Hive of the Saints* (Lincoln, NE: iUniverse, 2005), 145–46, is quoted by permission of the author.

LAMENTATION, POETRY, AND THE DOUBLE LIFE

Daniel Tobin

> For I am a passing guest, a sojourner like all my fathers.
> —Psalm 39:12

I. SOJOURNER

Noon, the low winter sun at its pinnacle, beginning of the afternoon visiting hour in Lutheran Medical intensive care, where my father continues to hold on to his life after nearly a week of capitulations and rallies, his cardiac function enumerated as if by a stock ticker on the machine beside his bed, and I'm still forty blocks away in front of Sally's Luncheonette waiting for my wife and mother-in-law to drive me to his bedside. I wait five more minutes, run inside to call a car service, only to find them waiting outside in the car, frantic themselves. They'd hit traffic on the Belt Parkway coming into Brooklyn from Floral Park, where my mother-in-law moved shortly before my wife's father passed away two years ago. From my old childhood apartment, it's about ten minutes to the hospital if you catch the lights along Third, or cut down to Ridge Boulevard to avoid the buses and double-parkers, the new construction on the Sixty-seventh Street Bridge. I don't bother to cancel the car service, but hop in, still feeling anxious as we pull out and head down the avenue. I try to calm myself, remembering that yesterday the guard let me stay at my father's bedside a little after the end of visiting hour.

I've been at the hospital morning, afternoon, and evening, every day since I discovered my father slumped in the foyer chair when I returned six days earlier from teaching at the January residency of the Warren Wilson MFA Program for Writers, my plane delayed because of fog caused by the unseasonable warmth. Reaching the four-room walk-up where my father lived with my mother for fifty years, I noticed the door was unlocked and slightly ajar so I could see the jamb, the dulled gold paint streaked tin-gray from where it used to stick, year after year, during my childhood. It still does. The apartment was dark, though to the right of the door I could see my father's friend John Gogarty look up at me from his niche just inside the kitchen.

"What's wrong?"

"He can't walk. He's been like this all day."

"Why didn't you call BRAVO?" Never one to confuse Bay Ridge Ambulance Volunteer Organization with the cable television Arts and Culture channel, my father always bristled at the code name, as though merely mentioning it might bring its necessity. Feet splayed, his head bent as though he were looking at something lost inside himself, traces of his red hair still noticeable in his navy-issue crew cut, my father mustered his predictable two cents, his voice slackened but still resonant with his years as a longshoreman on the Brooklyn docks after the war, as a bartender weekends at the American Legion.

"What's the matter? How are you feeling?"

"Lousy. Lousy."

John broke in: "I found him in the bathroom when I came up with the coffee this morning around ten. All day he wouldn't let me call. 'Wait till Danny gets home,' he said. So what could I do? It's all day, Danny, all day."

He was always stubborn about going to the doctor, about the best route out of the city (always over the Narrows Bridge, never through Manhattan), about not leaving Brooklyn since my mother died, though my brother and I both urged him to move near one of us. He wanted to make sure he was still in control, even if it meant killing himself, the way he'd always push each medical crisis almost beyond remedy—his collapse from a bleeding ulcer when I was ten, this past summer's heart failure at the family reunion. Then there's the more extensive history: sixty years of hard drinking and smoking despite his heart attack the year after I was born; despite the scalding as a child by his own alcoholic father; despite being abandoned at fifteen when his mother died, his father on the streets or in the drunk tank on Riker's; despite the series of car crashes driving home late nights from the bars; despite years of high blood pressure and emphysema, pills and patches, and, in the last two years, blood thinners that should never be mixed with alcohol. All day he was sitting in this chair, waiting for me, or death, whoever came first.

There was blood all over the bathroom floor, John told me, and John also told me how he carried him out to the foyer, and still again how they'd been waiting for me all day to come home. John was a stocky bull of a man, seven years older than my father, who had been smoking cigars and drinking since before Ireland became a republic in 1948. He was a good friend over the years, and an indispensable friend to my father since my mother died two years before.

"We thought you'd be earlier, Danny. It's been all day."

John's Northern brogue was undaunted by over fifty years in Brooklyn.

"The plane was delayed. Fog. I'm calling BRAVO," I said urgently.

"Danny, wait . . ." my father interjected, raising his head a little. It was as if my father's stubborn mantra were a painter's chisel scraping the veneer off my professorial calm, and I found myself screaming at him.

"What, are you nuts? This is serious. You can't walk." I paused for a second at the phone, mastering the dutiful son inside myself who would wait and wait, anything his father wanted, then dialed the number of the neighborhood emergency corps to rush my father to Lutheran.

"Wait, wait, wait, wait, wait." My father's voice sounded weak and disgusted, though more almost at my refusal to acquiesce to his demand than at his own condition. John had his hand on my father's shoulder and was talking to him soothingly.

"Danny's here now, Jerry, he knows what to do. They'll take care of you. You'll be alright now."

By the time I'd hung up the phone, I could hear my father muttering disgustedly to himself: "Oh, shit, oh shit," his speech slurred as though he'd been drinking, and shaking his head while his chest heaved to force air into his wasted lungs. I rubbed his shoulders. "They'll be here soon. We'll hear the siren."

When they wheeled him out that night, his blood pressure was ninety over fifty, though he stayed awake in the ambulance, and in the emergency room all that evening until he told me to go home and get some sleep. Now it is nearly noon and I'm walking as fast as I can without running down the hallway toward intensive care, Christine and her mother having dropped me off before they looked for a parking space. My father is in the far right room where they moved him two days ago from another part of the wing, but the first door nearest his room is locked. So I go through the next entry, walking intently across the room, only to find there is no bed where my father's was. It feels as if a trap door has just opened in my stomach. I look at the on-duty nurse, who recognizes me, then points toward the door I was unable to enter: "There he goes." There is my father in his bed, still hooked up to his machines, the image of a marionette stretched out after its performance, my father—bed and all—wheeled along by nurses. "We're taking him to critical care," one of the nurses says. "It's an improvement." Now I feel like the marionette, moved by invisible strings, dumbfounded at how my father has managed all his life to cheat death while courting it like a mistress.

I follow them to my father's new room, not far but on the other side of the building, but they stop me from coming in. "We have to set him up. Doctor Zak is waiting for you over there." I had met Dr. Zak earlier in the week—no-nonsense but, I decided, not without compassion. I knew he was doing the best for my father under difficult circumstances. Still recuperating from last summer's open-heart surgery, my father continued to smoke and drink despite taking Coumadin, a blood thinner that could become lethal when mixed with alcohol. That was my father's problem now, Coumadin toxicity leading to internal bleeding, complicated by his emphysema and the additional stress on his heart. It was Doctor Zak who had called last night to tell me that my father was in respiratory distress, that he could die unless they inserted the breathing tube again, though my father had adamantly refused another intubation. "No way," he managed despite the trauma to his vocal cords. Dr. Zak wanted my permission to overrule the Do-Not-Intubate order.

"Oh God," I'd blurted into the phone, "What do I do?" not of the doctor, nor of myself, but of some Other—an Absence hard as a fist. My whole body shook. Then I heeded my father's wish.

As I approach Dr. Zak he begins to explain, "We've finally managed to stop the bleeding in the digestive track. Also, he seems now to be able to breathe on the mask. So we have moved him to critical care, a little better than where he was. Not out of the woods, but better."

As Doctor Zak speaks I glance toward my father's new room and notice more nurses going in, some now standing in the doorway. Now one nurse walks over to where we are talking.

"Doctor Zak, I need you in Room 323."

"Is it important?" Doctor Zak signals with raised index finger that he'll be back shortly. Again, a wry smile moves across my mouth as I think about phoning my brother, who returned two days earlier to his family in Northampton. "He's amazing," I'm going to tell him with honest pride, despite my father's self-destructiveness, "an amazing man." And my brother will agree. As if on cue, Christine and her mother are walking down the hall.

"We had trouble finding you," my wife says.

"I bet. He's improved so they moved him here from intensive care. Can you believe it? He's amazing." Now Doctor Li walks over to us. I met her six days ago in the ER. Very competent, I felt at the time, very much in charge but warm, capable of dealing with frightened patients and anxious loved-ones. And I remembered my mother, hospitalized here with pneumonia, in delirium, convinced that people were trying to kidnap her: "Danny, you have to get me out of here. There going to take me to China." "Very embarrassing," my father remarked stoically; "those Chinese doctors can be very good." And my mother afterward saying, "I must have been hallucinating." That was three years ago, nine months before my mother died. I hadn't seen Doctor Li for the past few days, and now here she was at my side.

"Has anybody told you?"

"No."

"Your father has expired."

II. BREATH, SONG

> For all our days pass away under thy wrath, our years
> come to an end like a sigh . . . . and we fly away.
> —Psalm 90:9, 11

Expire, from the Latin *ex(s)-pirdre*, means "to breath out," the word itself born out of the body, yet rooted there as we are rooted in earth, though in everyday use it seems to have lost its connection to bodily life: *expired*, like a subscription to the newspaper, or a car insurance policy, or that witty but macabre grave that a friend told me about with its memorial sprouting a parking meter, its red flag reading "Expired." So, too, Doctor Li's "Your father has expired," the mechanized clock of the body run out, no coins to pay, no switch to turn to resume the time, another fifteen minutes, another hour or year, another lifetime. Twenty-five years ago my mother's mother, Nora, "expired." "Expired" is the word, it seems, doctors are taught to use at such moments, accurate but somehow sterilized of its origin in metaphor, at the same time almost too metaphorically precise—"to breathe out for the last time." To turn to the Psalms, however, is to enter a world in which the final breathing out of death enjoins another, more encompassing expiration—*ruach*, meaning "spirit, breath, wind," the creative power of YHWH. It is YHWH's breath that moves across the face of the waters in Genesis, bringing life, that can reanimate a desert of dry bones in Ecclesiastes, and it is that same *ruach* in Psalm 103 that makes "springs gush forth in the valleys," makes "the moon to mark the seasons," makes "wine to gladden the heart of man, oil to make his face shine." It is the breath, the wind, of God's creative imagination, the historical source of Romantic poetry's "correspondent breeze," the theism of ancient Israel morphing into the pantheism of Wordsworth through the complex undercurrents of Western culture. In this same psalm, however, YHWH also reveals his de-creative side:

> As for man, his days are like grass; he flourishes like a flower of the field;
> for the wind passes over it and it is gone. (Psalm 103:15–16)

Of all the many moods of the Psalms—grateful, ecstatic, laudatory, bitter, fiercely angry—it is this tone of lamentation I find supremely moving and compelling. Perhaps that is because by so vividly voicing his lament in the face of death the psalmist has managed to bespeak something universal in this most personal experience of loss. At the same time, most biblical scholars believe that in the Psalms we come closest to the thinking of ordinary Israelites: their exuberance at the harvest, their joy at the deliverance from enemies, their pleasure in daily and seasonal rituals, but also their longing for redress, their exasperation and cries at feeling abandoned by their God, their sufferings, and ultimately their need to reconcile themselves to death. In those passages when the human consciousness of death becomes dramatized, the Psalms achieve a transcendence that surpasses both the critical gaze of scholarly historical method and the untempered approbation of the true believer. Like all great poetry of suffering and mutability, the psalms of lament ground themselves in the physical details of life in order to express and ultimately dramatize an encounter with life's insignificance before forces that exceed our control—"the passivities of diminishment," Teilhard de Chardin called them—but I'm thinking still more of Job, of Oedipus, of Lear standing before Cordelia's lifeless body: "She's dead as earth," he cries out, and then he dies, too, in the moment dreaming vainly that she still breathes.

Nevertheless, over the course of the twentieth century, amid spectacles of brutality barely imaginable even to the psalmist, we have managed to efface the consciousness of our inherent passivity with a veneer of heroism. This is what the great French-Jewish phenomenologist Emmanuel Levinas found insidious in existentialist thought, and particularly in Heidegger's elucidation of *Dasein*—of human being as a kind of existence defined by the consciousness of death. For Heidegger, the fact of death permits a vista to open in which the human Will may act in the face of death's unsurpassable limit with freedom and virility. Levinas, in contrast, refuses the lure of Heidegger's idealism and shifts the guiding metaphor of his philosophy from a sublime but isolated gaze to one of relationship. For Levinas, life calls each of us to stand face to face before one another and enter into dialogue. And so, ultimately, the primary relation between human being and the world manifests itself as eros—lovers facing each other as equals—rather than the hero's solitary going forth into the unknown. "The Other," as Levinas calls all that lies outside us, finally eludes all of our efforts at understanding. So Levinas at once deepens our solitude and calls us to go out from it—an exodus at the heart of being. So, likewise, suffering is not a test that makes us stronger, nor can death be conquered by the Will. Instead, as he observes in *Time and the Other*, "in suffering there is an absence of all refuge. It is the fact of being directly exposed to being. It is made up of the impossibility of fleeing or retreating. The whole acuity of suffering lies in this impossibility of retreat" (69). To be fully exposed to being, of course, is to be fully exposed to death. In Levinas's subversion of Western idealist philosophy, I cannot help but hear an echo of the psalmist's cry, a desperate calling out toward YHWH who is the absolutely Other, the divine I AM who is at once the sufferer's personal God and beyond any human conception of personality:

> Hear my prayer, O Lord, let my cry come unto thee!
> Do not hide thy face from me in the day of my distress!
> Incline thy ear to me; answer me speedily in the day when I call!
>
> For my days pass away like smoke, and my bones burn like a furnace.
> My heart is smitten like grass, and withered; I forget to eat my bread.
> Because of my loud groaning my bones cleave to my flesh.
> I am like a vulture of the wilderness, like an owl of the waste places;
> I lie awake, I am like a lonely bird on the housetop.
> All the day my enemies taunt me, those who deride me make use of my
>   name for a curse.
> For I eat ashes like bread, and mingle tears with my drink,
> because of thy indignation and anger; for thou hast taken me up and
>   thrown me away.
> My days are like an evening shadow; I wither away like grass. (Psalm 102:1–11)

In justifying his exclusion of the World War I poets Siegfried Sassoon, Isaac Rosenberg, Wilfred Owen, and the like from the *Oxford Anthology of English Verse*, William Butler Yeats—a poet whose work I love as much as anyone's—remarked that passive suffering was not an acceptable theme for poetry. Obviously he had not been reading the Psalms. By then, however, Yeats had already long assumed the mask of the heroic, a stance that inclined him toward nostalgic ideas about the Irish race as well as conservative politics. If Yeats flirted with totalitarianism in his support of Colonel William Duffy and the Blue Shirts, then Ezra Pound became its whore in his delusions about Mussolini and his embrace of fascism as a heroic purgative to the mire he believed civilization had become. What affronts is not Pound's elitism, but a hero-worship that amounts to complicity with genocide: "The yidd is a stimulant and the goyim are cattle / in gt / proportion and to salable slaughter / with the maximum docility," Pound wrote in one of his expurgated Cantos. In our time, such dangerously misplaced desires for the transcendent— what we once called idolatry—have rendered the idea of transcendence itself suspect, even in some theological circles. Immanentist theology, it's called, an effort over the latter part of the last century to shake post-Nietzschean Christianity loose of its supernaturalism. Likewise, according to the dominant theoretical template in academic circles, all talk of poetry must be "historicized" and "politicized." In such views, the longing for transcendence is a dangerous longing—at best nostalgic, at worst intellectually and even spiritually bankrupt.

Yet the desire for transcendence reveals itself differently in the Psalms. Rather than otherworldly longing, or an obeisance before the god that is nothing other than the hero's alter ego or attendant lord, the psalmist's voice is the voice of justifiable complaint, of passionate speech driven to expression by a personal, historical, and ontological urgency:

> How long, O Lord? wilt thou forget me forever? How long wilt thou hide
>   thy face from me?
> How long must I bear pain in my soul, and have sorrow in my heart all
>   the day?
> How long shall my enemy be exalted over me?
> Consider and answer me, O Lord, my God. (Psalm 13:1–3)

Far from bowing down before some transcendent power, the speaker of Psalm 13 not only pleas but petitions to be heard, and requires a justification for God's absence, for his own apparent abandonment by God.

As such, the psalm at once subverts the dialogical structure of transcendence on which it is based—the speaker *has* been abandoned by YHWH whose name is I AM and who therefore is Being—even as it sustains that expectation by establishing a future, the only future imaginable, in which the speaker *is* answered. The desire for transcendence, brought on by acute suffering, becomes manifest as a call to relationship with God conceived of as radically Other. The trajectory, however, is "downward" rather than otherworldly, for YHWH is petitioned to respond in history, so transcendence becomes manifest as a relationship experienced in time. Rather than a denial of history, transcendence becomes realized within history as a longing cry. We hear that cry again in Psalm 6:

> O Lord, rebuke me not in thy anger, nor chasten me in thy wrath.
> Be gracious to me, O Lord, for I am languishing; O Lord heal me, for my
>   bones are sorely troubled.
> But thou, O Lord, how long?

For me, this doublespeak of petitioning God against his own absence is no Freudian delusion but constitutes the very essence of consciousness—of thought seeking an answer to its solitude, of thought seeking to establish a welcome for itself in Being through the act of speech. Philosophically speaking, this doublespeak requires a double vision, for though God is never seen, he is conceived of being at once utterly transcendent and immanent through his word, his inspiring breath. The God called out to by the psalmist is therefore also really Other—not merely the image of the speaker's desire, and therefore not wholly accountable to those desires. What does the psalmist ultimately desire? That God still breathes; that he exists, creates, and shapes history. What fear is implicit in the psalmist's cry? Incredible as it sounds, beyond any punitive action that God might take against the psalmist's presumptuous questions, he fears that God may have willed himself out of existence, or perhaps out of his existence as God. He fears that God has expired. The psalmist's speech, his song, is his effort to sing God back into Being, since for the time being, God has become mute, an absence, ineluctable, an emptiness at the heart of glory. The dialogical expectation of the psalm requires an eschatological answer, for God is both the primordial Poet and the ultimate audience on which both the psalmist's being and God's Being depend:

> Turn, O Lord, save my life; deliver me for the sake of thy steadfast love.
> For in death there is no remembrance of thee; in Sheol who can give
> thee praise? (Psalm 6:4–5)

Sheol, the land of the dead: a state akin to an eternal coma in which consciousness has all but expired: "What man can live and never see death? Who can deliver his soul from the power of Sheol?" (Psalm 90:48). And so the psalmist holds up to God, holds up before God's absent face, the reality of death itself as a kind of ontological bribe: You need me to remember you, just as I need for you not to forget me. The psalmist's song is the immanent dwelling for this mutual remembrance, the word's anticipatory *templum*. In the end the psalmist declares his hope: "The Lord accepts my prayer." It's as though, as Robert Hass says in "Santa Lucia," "the little song *transcend, transcend* could get us anywhere." The psalmist's lament is the eschatological song of reciprocal acknowledgment, of covenant, of call and response—YHWH calling on his people to be his people, the people calling on YHWH to be their God, and each awaiting the voice of the answerer. It is the same song uttered through the breath of being and called out Other to other, other to Other, without end, without expiration.

III. AFFLICTION

> Why are you cast down, O my Soul, and why are you
> disquieted within me?
> —Psalm 42:5

All day the painters scraped the four sides of the house, chip after brittle chip, the layers raining down until bare wood showed through. Christine and I had been up since their early morning arrival, every now and then looking out a window at this father and son who worked in tandem on high, sliding ladders. Later on, we watched them outstretched on our unmown lawn eating lunch. We heard the coarse rhythm of their tools along the old clapboards for hours as we worked inside on poems until, after small talk, fingers crossed for continued clear weather, they left in their truck. Maybe it was the small upheaval of this wanted change that wore us out, or the unrelenting heat, so that into the evening we flopped on the couch to watch TV. On the tube an aerial view of postwar Berlin, the bombed buildings flattened, jagged, unreeled in vivid presence on the bright square in front of us; and the documentary voice-over of Marlene Dietrich saying, "Who can believe in life after death, those hundreds of thousands killed, gone? Do you really believe they are all flitting around up there?" Later, we sat entranced by the *Nova* special "Runaway Universe," with its evidence of an expanding cosmos that reverses all expectations: no final cosmic implosion bringing everything back to origin; no eternal return of big bangs, expansions, and contractions oscillating through futureless futures; instead, an infinite cosmic extension that made my wife and me think of Walt Whitman's lines in *Leaves of Grass*:

> All goes onward and outward, nothing collapses,
> And to die is different from what anyone supposed, and luckier.

For one physicist interviewed, it's not luckier, but the worst end imaginable—whole galaxies spinning farther and farther apart, an unrelenting emptiness filling infinitely an infinite universe, the power of N raised to the never-ending. Unimaginable loneliness. Though what of the radical evidence they spoke of: only 5 percent of the universe, bodies, planets, stars, nebulae, galaxies, is sensible matter; the rest is "dark matter" and the more elusive "dark energy"—Einstein's "cosmic constant" true, so it turns out, filling the void with itself in its own image, present everywhere, visible nowhere, establishing itself out of the known and unknown. Invisibility. Omnipresence. God? Though God would require omnipotence as well—forgiveness and wrath—a dimension of the personal whether to create or destroy.

> *Christine*: We live in Flatland. We live in three dimensions, while the universe exists in twelve, at least, so the physicists say. Who's to presume consciousness ends, since consciousness is energy, and energy can't be destroyed?

Daniel: That sounds like *Star Trek*, the "Traveler" episode about the alien
who transforms from matter to energy and back again because energy
and matter and thought are really one.
Christine: Right, maybe that's our destiny.

And when the body dies is it liberated not to Sheol, but to Nirvana?
And was Ovid a proto-physicist, like Whitman, each metamorphosis
a redistribution of energy from human to flower, from god to human,
from human to god? And what of the resurrection, the risen body
transfigured beyond death? Does the dark energy build from our deaths
whole universes within our own, everlasting, and beyond our ken only
until we are called to them? Beyond the playful speculations of a tired
couple watching a science special before bed, Giuseppi Ungaretti's great
poem "Meditations on Death" bears witness to the question of ultimacy
that underlies a quiet evening's metaphysical insouciance:

> O sister of the shadow,
> blackest in strongest light,
> Death, you pursue me.

Here is death portrayed as a kind of dark energy, invisible, omni-
present, "blackest in strongest light," gaining on the speaker like a fleet-
footed god, bringing the final metamorphosis. There is a hauntedness in
Ungaretti's voice that resonates with the psalmist's when the horror of
death overwhelms him: "O that I had wings like a dove! I would fly away
and be at rest; / yea I would wander afar, I would lodge in the wilder-
ness" (Psalm 55:6–7). To lodge, to dwell, in a state of being unassailable
by death, that is what the psalmist desires, like the Italian poet. It is this
very hope that seems absent from another great poem of death, Philip
Larkin's "Aubade." Here is the first stanza:

> I work all day and get half-drunk at night.
> Walking at four to soundless dark, I stare.
> In time the curtain edges will grow light.
> Till then I see what's really always there:
> Unresting death, a whole day nearer now,
> Making all thought impossible but how
> And where and when I shall myself die.

Arid interrogation: yet the dread
Of dying, and being dead,
Flashes afresh to hold and horrify.

In Larkin's poem, Ungaretti's relentless pursuit and the psalmist's longing for flight settle into a psychic steady state, an *acedia* that cannot be reconciled or alleviated because here the psalmist's fear of metaphysical solitude has been realized. There is only the self, Descartes's personal pronoun thinking the ego into being; confronted with "restless death," all it can do for the rest of the poem is remove thought's assuaging answers. In one of the great metaphors of the later twentieth century, religion itself becomes "a vast moth-eaten musical brocade / created to pretend we never die." Death is "a special way of being afraid," Larkin affirms, and by owning death so relentlessly and unflinchingly Larkin's speaker portrays a world utterly without transcendence; without even the secular transcendence of Matthew Arnold's lovers at the end of "Dover Beach":

Slowly light strengthens, and the room takes shape.
It stands plain as a wardrobe, what we know,
Have always known, know that we can't escape,
Yet can't accept. One side will have to go.
Meanwhile telephones crouch, getting ready to ring
In locked-up offices, and all the uncaring
Intricate rented world begins to rouse.
The sky is white as clay, with no sun.
Work has to be done.
Postmen like doctors go from house to house.

At the end, there is no one for the speaker to be true to, there is only work that "has to be done" when the morning comes. Even the solaces of immanence—personal companionship, erotic love—have been curtailed to an almost pure isolation without prospect of appeal or appeasement, but for the postmen "like doctors" going from house to house. If we assume for a moment that the psalmist's longing exists perhaps unacknowledged in the poet's motivation to appeal to some "other," if only in the unquestioned desire to make the poem, then God's healing answer—the living breath of the divine Word—here has been reduced to the hope of a word from a distant friend or relation, though what's left in the mailbox may be only a solicitation or a bill.

Though at first it may appear coercive to find something of the psalmist's cry in Larkin's resolute refusal of transcendence, it seems to me obvious that poems like "High Windows," "Sad Steps," and "The Trees," to cite just a few other examples from Larkin's work, demonstrate a longing for transcendence equal to the psalmist's in urgency but abbreviated from explicitly religious expression by the poet's resolute skepticism. It likewise seems self-evident to me that the act of making a poem is a gesture outward toward "the other," even if the other is a wholly immanent audience. Of course, at the same time, language itself is other. The process of writing is a process of discovery—"no surprise in the writer, no surprise in the reader," Robert Frost said—and so it is a process of "othering" oneself in the making of a poem. Beyond such theoretical considerations, however, Larkin's speaker and the psalmist find common ground in their tone of lamentation because each—even Larkin's bourgeois speaker—has confronted in his own *acedia* the reality of affliction.

The spiritual sense of affliction subsumes and ultimately absorbs the physical meaning associated with the word, though physical pain in its most extreme manifestation epitomizes and embodies the unspeakable loss of spiritual abandonment that affliction signifies. As Simone Weil defines it, affliction is "an uprooting of life, a more or less attenuated equivalent of death, made irresistibly present to the soul by the attack or immediate apprehension of physical pain." Affliction, however, also entails the ego's ravaging before the felt prospect of its own nothingness, as well as the social degradation that attends this most diminished of states. Moreover, for Weil, affliction is "the great enigma of human life," for the allowance if not the agency that brings about affliction is finally God's. It is God's bargain with the devil to bring Job to utter desolation. As Weil observes, constrained by affliction, even Jesus cried out for consolation and believed himself "forsaken by the Father." A troublesome Jew, degraded and nailed in agony to the cross, he quotes Psalm 22:

My God, my God, why hast thou forsaken me? Why art thou so far from
   helping me, from the words of my groaning?
O my God, I cry by day, but thou dost not answer; and by night but find
   no rest. (Psalm 22:1–2)

By joining Jesus' own anguished cry to the psalmist's, the Gospel
writers sought to give what they saw as Christ's redemptive sacrifice
cultural as well as spiritual amplitude. But what is most haunting about
the scene in spite of all the iconography is Jesus' anonymity. In the
world's eyes he is just another criminal or slave. I have to travel back in
memory to my childhood and the crucifix that hung on the wall over
my parent's bed and look at the anguished face turned downward, the
crown of thorns, the gaunt body forever frozen in time like a figure on
Keats's urn, to recall what is probably my first image of affliction. Then
I have to look back through the warped glass of my own perceptions to
see my mother dead in the same bed, under the same cross, wasted by
years nursing a childhood wound she could not heal; nursing a sadness
that was for her unspeakable; and I have to go back to the room in
Lutheran Medical and try again to make out my father's unintelligible
rasps, then the mouthed silence after the breathing tube was removed,
and then the slack zero of his mouth in death. On the cross above both
these beds, Christ isn't saying anything. His pain is beyond speech. He
is the Word-Made-Flesh emptied into the body of flesh that has swal-
lowed the Word.

Years ago, reading Elaine Scarry's *The Body in Pain*, I recognized
intellectually at least that affliction is an impassible path; it is the world
brought to its limit as a world. "Physical pain," Scarry writes, "does not
simply resist language but actively destroys it, bringing about an imme-
diate reversion to a state anterior to language, to the sounds and cries a
human being makes before language is learned." Scarry's insight is one
implicitly addressed in Ellen Bryant Voigt's poem "Song and Story."
Weaving the Orpheus myth together with a story of a young girl strapped
to a mechanical crib who in her affliction cannot cry out, Voigt's poem
redefines the poet's work in the most compelling and urgent terms:

The one who can sing sings to the one who can't,
who waits in the pit, like Procne among the slaves,
as the gods decide how all such stories end.

In Voigt's poem, the child's affliction "unmakes" the world. Pain unmakes the world even though it pervades the world we inhabit, a terra incognita always encountered anew. It is the raw silence for which the poet, the singer, nevertheless must find words. Though unlike Voigt's poem the Psalms at times understand affliction as the outgrowth of sin—as Psalm 3 says, "There is no soundness in my flesh because of thy indignation"—at the deepest level of affliction sin reveals itself to be a subordinate rationale, a deflection from an unthinkable abandonment. Affliction is the world's cipher and origin, a wound and a womb where the world is made, or remade, in the poet's own answering efforts of reversal, the reversal that would answer the world's unmaking even if only in the form of the soul's most despairing lament:

> O Lord, my God, I call for help by day; I cry out in the night before thee.
> Let my prayer come before thee, incline thy ear to my cry!
> For my soul is full of troubles, and my life draws near to Sheol.
> I am reckoned among those who go down to the Pit; I am a man who has
> no strength,
> like one forsaken among the dead, like the slain that lie in the grave, like
> those whom thou dost remember no more for they are cut off from
> thy hand.
> Thou hast put me in the depths of the Pit, in the regions of dark and
> deep.
> Thy wrath lies heavy upon me, and thou dost overwhelm me with all
> thy waves.
> . . . .
> Is thy steadfast love declared in the grave, or thy faithfulness in Abaddon?
> Are thy wonders known in the darkness, or thy saving help in the land of
> forgetfulness?
> . . . .
> Afflicted and close to death from my youth up, I suffer thy terrors; I am
> helpless.
> Thy wrath has swept over me; thy dread assaults destroy me. (Psalm 88:1–7,
> 10–12, 15)

IV. WITNESS

> For a thousand years in thy sight are but as yesterday
> when it is past, or as a watch in the night.
> —Psalm 90:4

Twenty years ago I had the good fortune to be in the audience during Czeslaw Milosz's delivery of the Charles Eliot Norton Lectures at Harvard University. A graduate student in Religion and Culture at the time, I had only just earnestly begun seeking a life in poetry by taking classes and joining workshops. I had picked up *Bells in Winter* the year before, and still remember reading it on the "R" train from Brooklyn to my job as a clerk at the Doubleday Bookstore in Lower Manhattan—work I had sought against my parent's wishes that I begin a management training program at Merrill-Lynch. The second son of a blue-collar family, I was expected to find a well-paying job, preferably in business, though it was my mother's dream that I should become, of all things, a dentist. The priesthood would have been a worthy choice as well, and indeed for a time I contemplated that vocation, majoring in religion at Iona College—"that blue-collar Roman school," as one graduate professor described it. Now I sat in stately Memorial Hall Theater, a would-be doctor of theology and culture who would be lured away from that calling as well. Though proud that I attended Harvard, my parents would have preferred the "B" School and an MBA.

Nevertheless, there I was, listening to one of the great poets of the twentieth century expound not only on an art that despite its allure seemed impossibly beyond my birthright, but on religion, politics, European literature, the nature of Western culture across the axis of Rome and Byzantium, past and future, as well as on the unthinkably brutal history of the twentieth century told from the perspective of one who had witnessed it and survived. I knew then, however awkward I might have felt as a "blue-collar scholar" among those who seemed to me economically and culturally chosen, that I was by any reasoned account privileged both to be where I was at that moment and not to have been born into the cauldron of want and atrocity that contains much of the world. The following year, when *The Witness of Poetry* appeared in print, I underlined whole passages, emphasized still more urgent ideas with checks and stars and, occasionally, my own scrawled commentary. Here is one of Milosz's observations to which I continue to return:

> The twentieth century is a purgatory in which the imagination must manage without the relief that satisfies one of the essential needs of the human heart, the need for protection. Existence appears as ruled by necessity and chance, with no divine intervention: until recently God's hand used to bring help to pious rulers and to punish sinful rulers. But now even the idea of Progress, which was nothing else but Providence secularized, no longer provides any guarantee.

More than twenty years since I first read these words, Milosz's assessment of the situation of poetry strikes me as no less remarkably trenchant and germane. If faith in divine intervention against the often cruel operations of history and blind fate retains any currency, it does so more often than not without the assurance of a rite that unequivocally galvanizes the soul. Indeed, when a particular cultus reaches such intensity, even within the circles of traditional religious practice, one begins to fear that Freud and Marx may have been right about the inherently delusive nature of religion. On the other hand, as Milosz's observation equally reminds us, the cult of Progress offers no appeasement and smacks of an equally dubious determinism and triumphalism. Far from improving the plight of those left behind, the immense strides in technology that have shaped the world since I sat in that theater dedicated to sublime thought and expression have done nothing to change the sources of oppression and brutality in the human heart, the same heart that longs for protection—political, economic, metaphysical, or otherwise. Given this circumstance, and the degree of injustice and violence that manifests itself daily in our global village, it strikes me that one could understand Milosz as optimistic when he called our present state a purgatory. There is an end to purgatory, but there is no end to affliction.

From this perspective, the Psalms seem removed from us, precisely because however afflicted the speaker may be, the expectation of dialogue that pervades and underwrites the psalmist's lament negates

YHWH's absence by calling on God's presence eschatologically: How long, O Lord? There will be protection; the suffering will end. Above all, the expectation of cosmic or divine protection requires a kind of metaphysical waiting. If one were to believe my old professor at Iona College, Brother Mark Hunt, then despite the psalmist's intense affliction, it is God's *chesed*, His "steadfast love," that finally supervenes, and so faith overcomes even utter disintegration:

> By the waters of Babylon, there we sat down and wept when we
>   remembered Zion.
> On the willows there we hung up our lyres.
> For there our captors required of us songs, and our tormentors, mirth,
>   saying "Sing us one of the songs of Zion!"
>
> How shall we sing the Lord's song in a foreign land?
> If I forget you O Jerusalem, let my right hand wither!
> Let my tongue cleave to the roof of my mouth, if I do not remember you,
>   if I do not set Jerusalem above my highest joy. (Psalm 137:1–6)

In the first stanza, one of the most beautiful and famous in all the Psalms, song is refused as an action efficacious of faith, for it has become a tool of irony alone, irony that bespeaks and intensifies Israel's disintegration not only as a community of tribes and a cultus but possibly as a civilization. Whether in protest against the jeers of their captors, or in response to a world-altering loss, Israel has been silenced in the most radical way. The second stanza, however, performs the redemptive reversal of that silence back into speech, into song, through the interpolation of the essential question—the question of existence. Song enacts itself in self-interrogation and thereby enacts the psalmist's reversal of the negation of being through a surpassing moment of self-witness. At this moment the psalm becomes something more than the lament of an individual caught in a historical atrocity, more than the collective voice of an oppressed people in shambles, more even than the human voice transmuted into a kind of exemplary subjectivity, a befitting emblem for all the lost of history. Beyond all these, the psalmist's question manifests the voice of the infinite in search of its own infinitely assuaging being, for without song there is no divine audience and therefore no covenant, no call and response, no infinite at once transcending and subtending the primary relationship of being to itself: I AM therefore *you are*, *you are* so therefore I MUST BE. This is the essential ontological logic of the Psalms, perhaps of all song, all making, and the indispensable presumption of language. Here the song or word that creates, that "lets be," is a question, not an imperative: not exactly Rainer Maria Rilke's *Gesang ist Dasein*, "song is existence," where Orpheus's song emerges as a pure affirmation, the mythopoeic, creational naming of Genesis lodged in the mouth of the Greek god, but song that rises out of being's profound negation by history, the very history perceived to be shaped by YHWH, the source of being itself.

About the same time that I enrolled in Brother Hunt's class on the Psalms, I found myself listening occasionally to Don McLean's benchmark album *American Pie*. One song on the flip side from the album's classic track was a version of Psalm 137 sung a capella by McLean, his voice resonant and velvety, lifting and diminishing beautifully with the psalm's moving lamentation and its desire for endurance through hardship. What McLean's version left out, what is often left out of an innocent reading of the Psalms, is the intensity of the retributive violence YHWH is called upon to inflict on behalf of the afflicted:

> Remember, O Lord, against the Edomites the day of Jerusalem, how they
>   said, "Raze it, raze it!
> Down to its foundations!"
> O daughter of Babylon, you devastator! Happy shall be he who requites
>   you with what you have done to us!
> Happy shall he be who takes your little ones and dashes them against the
>   rock! (Psalm 137:7–9)

In Brother Hunt's class, such extreme calls for revenge were glossed over, and it's no surprise that the same pop singer who crooned about "the devil laughing in the dark" when Buddy Holly died might elide Psalm 137's brutal crescendo. This is the God witnessed in Job's magisterial theophany, a God who exists outside human bounds and human morality and who may act in history as he sees fit, whether to rally to avenge the tribal covenant or to vent his wrath on the chosen. It is this kind of divine portrayal that led Carl Jung in *Answer to Job* to conclude that evil must be seen as constitutive of the divine archetype itself. Let God "break the teeth in their mouth," Psalm 58 says of the wicked. In *Violence and the Sacred*, René Girard envisions humanity's urge to exact revenge and to displace its innate impulse toward violence in a scapegoat as the origin of all religion, indeed of civilization itself. For Girard, we need a version of "malevolent transcendence" so the violence that would destroy a community's social fabric might be sanctioned divinely and finally projected onto the Other. Against those who might see the call to violence in the Psalms as a subversion of their understanding of the sacred, and against those who on the contrary innocently gloss over this disturbing attribute of the psalmist's world, I would argue that the psalmist's voice achieves credibility by being so unguarded, by giving range to the most disturbing as well as to the most exalted of human impulses.

In Psalm 74, which is described in the Revised Standard Version of the Bible as a prayer for deliverance from national enemies, the psalmist petitions God to "have regard for thy covenant; for the dark places of the land are full of habitations of violence." Tempering an at times *Clockwork Orange* brand of divine "ultra-violence" in the Psalms is their call to social justice, a call that might be seen as a warning to God: "Help your people, or your people will perish." YHWH is, to use a theological term, a *mysterium tremendum*—a tremendous mystery, the other which is Absolutely Other: the Voice that addresses Moses on Sinai and Job in the whirlwind. But what happens when the acknowledged humanity of Psalms—its longing for transcendence and justice as well as its nascent violence—confronts a world devoid of justice and constructed from false idols of transcendence? That is the world Milosz called to mind in his Norton lectures, the world of the Holocaust, another kind of *tremendum*, as Jewish theologian Arthur Cohen defines it: the comprehensive model of brutality that ends in the total humiliation of human being. What place do the Psalms have in this world, or in the world that comes after? "After Auschwitz, no poetry," Theodor Adorno famously remarked. Yet there is Paul Celan's "Psalm":

No one kneads us again
out of earth and clay,
no one breathes
back our dust.
                No one.

Praised be to you, No one.
For your sake
we shall blossom
brokenly to you.

A nothing we were,
are, shall remain,
blossoming: the Nothing,
the No One's rose.

With our pistil
soul-radiant,
with our stamen
wasted of heaven,

our corona red
with the bloody word
that we sang
over, O over

the thorn.[1]

A survivor of Auschwitz, Paul Celan lost his entire family to its ovens before producing some of the greatest poetry of the latter part of the twentieth century before he committed suicide in 1970. An admirer of Heidegger's philosophy despite Heidegger's silence regarding his own membership in the Nazi Party, Celan's work inhabits the ontological antiworld that came into being after the self-immolation of a prior Western idealism, the greatest poetic expression of which might be Rilke's "Duino Elegies": "Who, if I cried out, would hear me among the angel's / hierarchies?" The answer after Auschwitz is "No one." With its central metaphor derived from the tradition of Western love poetry stemming back to Song of Solomon and carrying forward to Rilke, the negation of Celan's "Psalm" can't be underestimated. Its voice, as if from the very nadir of cosmic affliction, raises itself out of "the Death-World," to use a term coined by Edith Wyschogrod in *Spirit in Ashes*. In the Death-World, the wholesale extermination of persons has been accomplished by fiat, tuned to a pristine technology, and underwritten by a self-justifying myth born, as it were, out of the demonic perversion of the symbols that have shaped Western culture. The utopian paradise of Aryanism, like all brands of racial engineering, requires the apocalyptic eradication of the "scapegoated" Other. So in an utterly God-corrupted, God-forsaken universe, "Psalm" succeeds in speaking the unspeakable, in singing the unsingable. It breathes out from the desolation of omnipotent being an answer to God's silence with its own "crimson word" that aspires to transcendence beyond the expired image of God and in spite of an afflicted cosmos consumed by Malevolence and raised to the power of No-God at all.

V. DWELLING AND THE DOUBLE LIFE

> God gives the desolate a home to dwell in.
> —Psalm 68:6

That afternoon in late August five months before my father died, I strapped myself into the stiffly padded seat across from his stretcher in the ambulance hired to take him from Cooley-Dickinson Hospital in Northampton, Massachusetts, to Brigham and Women's Hospital in Boston. Since early July and his first attack at a family reunion in East Durham, New York, I had spent the better part of the summer living in hotels near hospitals where doctors tried to stabilize his condition. It was in Hudson Hospital that the doctor refused to send him home to his Brooklyn apartment—his heart so weak he could no longer make the stairs. Schooled, as he used to say, at the College of Hard Knocks, my father wasn't prone to crying, but he cried that afternoon, holding onto my hand and my brother's as though we were all that kept him from falling off the edge of the world. We were.

Later that week, stabilized, an oxygen tank wheeled alongside of him with its translucent tube wrapped like a cheap Halloween mask around his ears, he climbed into my brother's minivan to spend what he hoped would be two weeks recuperating outside Northampton while I took care of things in the Brooklyn apartment and my wife waited for me back in Wisconsin. He looked forward to seeing his grandchildren, but looked forward more to getting back to Brooklyn, to resuming the habits of his life—breakfast at Sally's Coffee Shoppe; Tuesday meetings at St. Anselm's Young at Heart; lunch at Pegasus or Hinsch's luncheonette; lighting candles at church; his afternoon Scotch at Muse's Bar; then back to the lonely apartment to drink more, and smoke, and watch TV before going to bed. Even though my mother had died nearly a year earlier, he still hid the cigarettes and bottles out of habit. Habit was what kept my father going and what was killing him. And he vowed to get back to Brooklyn, even after the second attack at my brother's house that brought another emergency call, and left him unconscious among my frantic brother and his wife, his screaming grandchildren, everyone waiting for the ambulance. Revived from the dead, kept alive by transfusions of plasma, fed intravenously, his heart monitored by radar, a respirator tube growing from his mouth like a plastic branch sprouting a long transparent vine, he jotted instructions to my brother and me, pad after pad reduced to a thin line of glue, his stubby pencils blunting with the words: *How are the kids? When is the tube coming out? When can I go back to Brooklyn?* And after they excavated the tube from his throat and the doctor told him that his one chance was surgery, he left for the sojourn of open-heart surgery, his head packed in ice as they rerouted his blood, replaced the lapsed valve, reconstructed the aorta; then days of living in Sheol, swollen, thrashing in bed, the heart stronger now but the consciousness in question; and then the waking, weeks of therapy; and then, refusing anything else, back to Brooklyn, to the old apartment two flights up now scaled one step at a time; to the one place he believed he could be himself; to "the same four walls," he'd say when I'd call, the vow accomplished: back to his home.

It was after I'd left my hotel in Boston near the hospital, resumed my teaching position and the rhythm of the school year, after he had been rushed in trauma again to Lutheran Medical in Brooklyn, after the wake and the long ride following the hearse to Resurrection Cemetery, that

I realized the judgment—"He's amazing"—referred most profoundly to my father's desire to dwell according to his own terms in the world; that whatever habits and compulsions he felt—even the destructive ones—were efforts at maintaining a world against the inevitability of loss. A great-grandson of the Irish Famine who himself had witnessed and participated in the whirlwind of twentieth-century history, he lived during a period when physical pain had become, according to Czeslaw Milosz, "a most simple touchstone for reality." It is the unavoidable awareness of pain's pervasiveness—of affliction—that at once heightens our perceptions of the individual's solitude and prompts a renewed appreciation for the web of relationships that situate everyone, indeed everything, in being. Even the accoutrements of my father's illness—the tubes, the intravenous, the electrodes signaling invisibly to stations down the hall—made manifest, made visible, the web of dependencies that sustain us even in health. It is as though disease, horrible as it is, reveals the invisible patterns of affinity which enable each one of us to exist at all and to which each one is called to participate according to one's chances, labors, and intents. Each one of us lives a double life, the life of one's sole self and the other invisible life we sometimes awaken to that binds us each to each, other to other, as if all things are held in relationship by some dark energy transcending both our knowledge and our mastery to name it.

In the Jewish mysticism called Kabbalah, this darkness at the heart of being is called Ayin, "nothingness" or "the Boundless," because it transcends every conception even as it pervades all existence—invisible, omnipresent, like the primordial energy that the *Nova* scientists claimed filled all space and that accelerates the expanding universe, though perhaps it's dangerous to confuse spiritual and physical categories even through a simile, as if the contemporary mind considering such issues were hopelessly split. One wants to retreat from the vexatious confusions of "creation science," from the coldly mechanical cosmos of scientific positivism, to avert one's eyes from the bumper sticker in the shape of a fish that reads "Jesus," from the bumper sticker in the shape of the same fish that reads "Darwin." What has speculation of this kind to do with lamentation, pain, affliction, the causes of which beg for answers more assuaging than grandiose abstractions or New Age flakiness? "The one who can sing sings to the one who can't," Ellen Bryant Voigt's poem reminds us, and so she sings *for* the one who can't. Just so, Celan's "Psalm" sings as if in the impossible voice of the obliterated. Both poems predicate their singing on the assumption that a bridge can be made across the gulf that exists between the fragile nature of our material-ity and the object of a longing that, however despaired of, nonetheless would offer an appeasement that surpasses the laws of physical neces-sity. Voigt's gods in "Song and Story" are as capricious as chaos itself; and Celan's transcendent "No One" signifies a vacuum in the heart of omnipotence. Still, both presume the ultimate dialogue underlying the psalmist's spiritual urgency:

> As a hart longs for flowing streams, so my soul longs for thee, O God!
> My soul longs for God, for the living God. When shall I come and behold
> the face of God?
> Day and night my tears have been my bread, while men say to me
> continually, "Where is your God?" (Psalm 42:1–3)

These lines from Psalm 42 constitute the perfect evocation of long-ing not merely as a profound emotion but as an act of metaphysical construction. God is not present; otherwise there would be no affliction as well as no song. The spiritual architecture of longing involves making a bridge between the immanent realm of the singer and the transcen-dent realm in which the singer's longing presumably will be satisfied. It begins in analogy, metaphor: "As a hart longs for flowing streams. . . ." But it would extend to an order of reality that eludes metaphor, even though metaphor is all we have to describe its existence: "the face of God." No one can see the face of God and live, so the sweep of longing extends from the created to the uncreated. It is a bridge across the gulf of being to a still greater emptiness, and yet it is that greater emptiness that paradoxically secures the psalmist's song.

As Wallace Stevens observed in *The Necessary Angel* where he invokes Simone Weil, poetry in our time entails de-creation, the act of making something pass from the created into the uncreated. Another way of stating this is to say that because poetry is liminal, at once partaking of the senses and effacing them, it stands in for or anticipates an order to life consonant with an abiding and infinite Regard without denying the world's fragility and finitude. Poetry, as a witness to worldliness and a longing for what might assuage it, embodies the double life of our common human circumstance as beings in between the dust that we are and the divinity to which we would aspire. The poetry of longing would therefore inscribe a formal arc outward from the lived life into the uncreated. If the poet's song could wholly satisfy its longing and attain its desire, it would transform itself into the "foreign song" of Stevens's "Of Mere Being," its gold-feathered bird alive inside an order of reality that transcends human meaning and human feeling, but not because that reality is inhuman. To adapt Dante's pivotal verb, to satisfy longing of this kind would be to "transhumanize" song according to the heavenly registers. Instead, we are left with a formal arc that returns us to the sole self and its intimations of greater life. We follow the ecstatic course of consciousness exemplified in Keats's "Ode to a Nightingale": first solitude and heartache, then the desire to dissolve consciousness through a Bacchic disordering of the senses, then the flight of art with its delusion of union ("Already with Thee!"), then the plummet back to earth and darkness to confront the reality of pain and death, and the solitary mind's desire for death as an answer to solitude, then finally, inevitably, the mind's return back to the "sole self" now disoriented from its inner sojourn, its would-be journey beyond its own solitude. And it's not that Keats wishes to leave the flesh behind in favor of the golden realms of spirit. The desire is to transfigure flesh and spirit—that double life at the core of human consciousness—into a more rarified and subtle incarnation. Both Stevens's gold-feathered bird and Keats's nightingale point us toward scales of being at once resistant to human language and demanding of embodiment in human terms.

"Be still before the Lord, and wait patiently for him," Psalm 37 advises with its Zen-like sense of equanimity, so different from the psalms of lamentation, with their acute awareness of affliction. Here, too, however, there is longing, though now the agitated ecstasy exemplified in Keats's "Ode to a Nightingale" has been quelled to the selfless acceptance and transparency of being and its passing that we find in "To Autumn." It is the most fully realized instance of Keats's "Negative Capability"—the ideal poet's aptitude for waiting in doubt without anxiety, without the anxious grasping after more that Augustine defined as concupiscence, his phenomenological proof of original sin. At the same time, lest it devolve into quietism, waiting requires contention. These antithetical moods are present everywhere in the psalms and at times they mingle, as in the poetry of Gerard Manley Hopkins:

> Thou art indeed just, Lord, if I contend
> With thee; but, sir, so what I plead is just.
> Why do sinners' ways prosper? and why must
> Disappointment all I endeavor end?

Echoing the psalms, Hopkins's "terrible sonnet" asks for nothing less than a biblical theodicy, God's own self-justifying revelation before the creaturely self. Regardless of the reader's own faith in an answer, Hopkins's longing is the reader's insofar as he articulates the ultimacy of such questions for human beings and not just for himself. It seems to me that the secular portrayal of what is at stake in Hopkins's poem may be found in Elizabeth Bishop's "In the Waiting Room." Here, the child Elizabeth's waiting for her Aunt Consuelo in the dentist's office unfolds without reference to any vertical axis of faith whatsoever. It is February 1918. We are placed entirely within the horizontal time-line of history. The world of Bishop's dentist's office is a world devoid of transcendence in any traditional sense. It is a purely immanent spot of time. Nevertheless, the little girl's inner journey beyond the self by which she will realize her particular selfhood is spurred by a sudden, albeit restrained, revelation of suffering:

> Suddenly from inside,
> came an *oh!* of pain
> —Aunt Consuelo's voice—
> not very loud or long.
> I wasn't at all surprised;

even then I knew she was
a foolish timid woman.
I might have been embarrassed,
but wasn't. What took me
completely by surprise
was that it was *me*:
my voice, in my mouth.
Without thinking at all
I was my foolish aunt,
I—we—we falling, falling,
our eyes glued to the cover
of the *National Geographic*,
February, 1918.

The sudden vertigo the child experiences attends upon the oblitera-
tion of the illusion of individual selfhood. It is as if the invisible strings
that connect us all had suddenly manifested themselves in a supreme
moment of identification. As in "Ode to a Nightingale," the experience
of self-surpassing is both abrupt and ephemeral, and occasioned by the
recognition of pain and mortality. Though it does not make reference
to anything outside the purely temporal or appeal to the eternal I AM,
"In the Waiting Room" does prompt the question of ultimate concern,
the question of existence itself: "Why should I be my aunt / or me, or
anyone?" In this essential respect Bishop's waiting room becomes the
world, the world where longing defines the human circumstance and
where we wait either with or without hope.

CODA: AN AFTERLIFE

Six months to the day after my father died, I received a letter informing
me of the poet Tom Andrews's death of a blood disease, Thrombotic
thrombocytopenic purpura. He was only forty. I had met Tom during
the January Residency at Warren Wilson, though I had read his poems
years earlier and had been impressed by their spare beauty as well as
their wise and compassionate sense of life. I knew of his hemophilia,
as well as his passion for racing motorcycles, from reading his memoir,
Codeine Diary—hemophilia and motorcycle racing: a combination of
facts that still seems to me to a defiant fusion of chance and intention, a

marvelous affirmation of life in the face of incipient affliction. Though I didn't know him well enough to call myself a friend, we hit it off over the course of the week, and I felt comfortable with his soft-spoken nature, his friendly and generous demeanor, as well as his wicked sense of humor. Near the end of the residency, we collaboratively led a workshop that afterward we both agreed was among the best either of us had experienced in our teaching lives. Though Tom had recently given up his position at Purdue University and moved to Greece, we looked forward to meeting again.

Three months earlier, after my father's death and before Tom's, I received word that another friend had lost his four-year-old daughter to a sudden illness. Then a colleague's college-age daughter died. Prior to these losses, but within the relatively short span of the past two years, I could add many others to the list: my father-in-law, my mother, a cousin's husband, a string of colleagues. Beyond them the numbers redouble, and redouble again into infinity. As well as being personal, death is nothing if not exponential. How, then, can poetry stand up to such loss; or, to quote Milosz again: "What is poetry that does not save nations, or people?" Yes, or the lost, or the forgotten, or the daily extinctions, or the dwindling environment? The universe is accelerating, expanding onward and outward, though all around we perceive things collapsing. To the naked eye gazing from the naked self it doesn't seem, as Whitman said, luckier. If God exists, we may have to abandon the idea of God's omnipotence, to embrace a God as weak as or weaker than ourselves, and still greater in that weakness if one can take seriously the Greek word *kenosis*, signifying the self-emptying of the divine into the cosmos. God's ecstasy is the creation. Perhaps our ecstasy is finally to embody our own inevitable self-emptying in ways the most vital of our poetry strives to imagine. For this there is longing, and the dead talking back to us in our own secret voices, like Tom Andrews in his poem "At Burt Lake"—the dead in their afterlife of lives in-dwelling, to which I must give the last word:

> To disappear into the right words
> and to be their meanings . . .

October dusk.
Pink scraps of clouds, a plum-colored sky.
The sycamore tree spills a few leaves.
The cold focuses like a lens . . .

Now night falls, its hair
caught in the lake's eye.

Such clarity of things. Already
I've said too much . . .

                  Lord,
language must happen to you
the way this black pane of water,
chipped and blistered with stars,
happens to me.

NOTES

1. My translation.

CONTRIBUTORS' NOTES

ROBERT A. AYRES received his master's in theological studies from Virginia Theological Seminary and his MFA in creative writing from the Warren Wilson Program for Writers. His poems have appeared in literary journals and anthologies. A native of San Antonio, he currently lives in Austin. He manages his family's ranchlands in the Hill Country and in the Davis Mountains of West Texas.

DAVID CITINO (1947–2005) published twelve books, including *Book of Appassionata: Collected Poems, Broken Symmetry,* and *The Weight of the Heart,* and served as coeditor of *The Bible as Literature,* 5th edition. The winner of numerous awards for his writing and teaching, he taught at Ohio State University for more than thirty years.

ENID DAME (1943–2003) published several books, including *Anything You Don't See, Lilith and Her Demons, On the Road to Damascus, Maryland,* and *Stone Shekhina.* She won a Many Mountains Moving literary award, as well as two Puffin Foundation grants and a New York State CAPS fellowship. She taught at the New Jersey Institute of Technology and Rutgers University.

MADELINE DEFREES is the author of numerous books of poetry, including *Blue Dusk: New and Selected Poems, 1951–2001,* for which she won the Lenore Marshall / *The Nation* Prize. She taught for many years at the University of Montana and currently lives in Seattle.

LYNN DOMINA is the author of a collection of poetry, *Corporal Works,* as well as reference books on Leslie Marmon Silko and Lorraine Hansberry. She currently lives in the western Catskill region of New York.

JILL ALEXANDER ESSBAUM is the author of *Heaven* (University Press of New England, 2000) and *Harlot* (No Tell Books, 2007). She divides her time between the United States and Switzerland.

ANGIE ESTES is the author of three books of poems, most recently *Chez Nous* (Oberlin College Press, 2005). Her second book, *Voice-Over* (2002), won the FIELD Poetry Prize and the Alice Fay di Castagnola Prize from the Poetry Society of America. Her first book, *The Uses of Passion* (1995), received the Peregrine Smith Poetry Prize. She has received fellowships in poetry from the National Endowment for the Arts, the National Endowment for the Humanities, the Woodrow Wilson Foundation, the California Arts Council, and the Ohio Arts Council and was awarded a Pushcart Prize.

DIANE GLANCY is a professor at Macalester College, where she has taught Native American literature and creative writing. Currently she is on a sabbatical, and in 2008 and 2009 she will hold the Richard Thomas Chair at Kenyon College. Her latest books are *In-Between Places* (essays) and *Asylum in the Grasslands* (poems), both from the University of Arizona Press; *Rooms: New and Selected Poems*, from Salt Publishers; and *The Dance Partner* (stories of the Ghost Dance), from Michigan State University Press.

JANET McCANN is the author of several books, including *Pascal Goes to the Races* and *Emily's Dress*. She is the coeditor of *Francis and Clare in Poetry: An Anthology*, *Place of Passage: Contemporary Catholic Poetry*, and other anthologies. She teaches at Texas A&M University.

ALICIA OSTRIKER is a prize-winning poet, critic, and midrashist whose work appears in many Jewish anthologies and journals and whose previous writing on the Bible includes *Feminist Revision and the Bible* (1992), *The Nakedness of the Fathers: Biblical Visions and Revisions* (1994), and the preface to an edition of *The Five Scrolls* (2000). Her essay on Psalms appears in *For the Love of God: The Bible as an Open Book* (2007). Ostriker is professor emerita of Rutgers University and leads midrash writing workshops in the United States and abroad.

CARL PHILLIPS is the author of nine books of poems, most recently *Quiver of Arrows: Selected Poems, 1986–2006*. His honors include the Kingsley Tufts Poetry Award and fellowships from the Guggenheim Foundation and the Library of Congress. In 2006, he was elected a Chancellor to the Academy of American Poets.

PATTIANN ROGERS has published thirteen books; the most recent is *Wayfare* (Penguin, 2008). She is the recipient of two NEA grants, a Guggenheim Fellowship, a 2005 Literary Award in Poetry from the Lannan Foundation, and five Pushcart Prizes, among other awards. She is currently on the faculty of the MFA Program in Writing at Pacific University. She has two sons and three grandsons and lives with her husband, a retired geophysicist, in Colorado.

CATHERINE SASANOV is the author of two volumes of poetry, *Traditions of Bread and Violence* (Four Way Books) and *All the Blood Tethers* (Northeastern University Press); a chapbook, *What's Left of Galgani* (Franciscan University Press); and the libretto for the theater piece *Las Horas de Belén: A Book of Hours*, commissioned by Mabou Mines. She lives in Boston.

DANIEL TOBIN is the author of four books of poems—*Where the World Is Made, Double Life, The Narrows*, and *Second Things*—as well as the critical study *Passage to the Center: Imagination and the Sacred in the Poetry of Seamus Heaney*; he also edited the anthology *The Book of Irish American Poetry from the Eighteenth Century to the Present*. Among his awards are the Discovery/*The Nation* Award, the Robert Penn Warren Award, the Robert Frost Fellowship, the Katherine Bakeless Nason Prize, and a creative writing fellowship from the National Endowment for the Arts. Widely published in journals, his work also has been anthologized in *The Bread Loaf Anthology of New American Poets, The Norton Introduction to Poetry*, and elsewhere. He is chair of the Department of Writing, Literature, and Publishing at Emerson College.

INDEX

INDEX OF PSALMS CITED